KNIT
step by step

KNIT
step by step

Vikki Haffenden and
Frederica Patmore

Previously published in *The Knitting Book*

DK

LONDON, NEW YORK, MUNICH,
MELBOURNE, AND DELHI

DK INDIA
Assistant Editor Aditi Batra
Assistant Art Editors Tanya Mehrotra, Aastha Tiwari
Senior Art Editor Anchal Kaushal
Managing Editor Glenda Fernandes
Managing Art Editor Navidita Thapa
CTS Manager Sunil Sharma
DTP Designer Satish Chandra Gaur

DK UK
Senior Designer Pamela Shiels
Project Editor Kathryn Meeker, Laura Palosuo
Managing Editor Penny Smith
Managing Art Editor Marianne Markham
Senior Jacket Creative Nicola Powling
Production Editor Siu Chan
Senior Production Controller Seyhan Esen
Creative Technical Support Sonia Charbonnier
Publisher Peggy Vance

DK US
Editor Margaret Parrish
Senior Editor Shannon Beatty
Consultant Jennifer Wendell

Material first published in the United States in *The Knitting Book*, 2011
This edition first published in 2012 by DK Publishing
375 Hudson Street, New York, New York 10014

12 13 14 15 16 10 9 8 7 6 5 4 3 2 1
001—179846—August/2012

Published in Great Britain by Dorling Kindersley Ltd.

A catalog record for this book is available from the Library of Congress.

ISBN: 978-0-7566-9271-1

DK books are available at special discounts when purchased in bulk for
sales promotions, premiums, fund-raising, or educational use.
For details, contact: DK Publishing Special Markets, 375 Hudson Street,
New York, New York 10014 or SpecialSales@dk.com.

Printed and bound by South China Printing Co. Ltd., China

Discover more at www.dk.com

CONTENTS

INTRODUCTION

This book is a comprehensive guide to a wealth of knitting skills. From basic techniques to those for more experienced knitters, there really is something for every knitter here. Each technique is explained with easy-to-follow, step-by-step instructions and delightfully clear color photographs. More unusual stitch structures are shown in step-by-step detail and related techniques are cross-referenced.

If you are a beginner, the choice of rich and exciting patterns in the swatch library will quickly tempt you to put your newly learned techniques into practice. For the adventurous and the more advanced, this book will provide you with the skills to consider incorporating individual design details into your knitted projects.

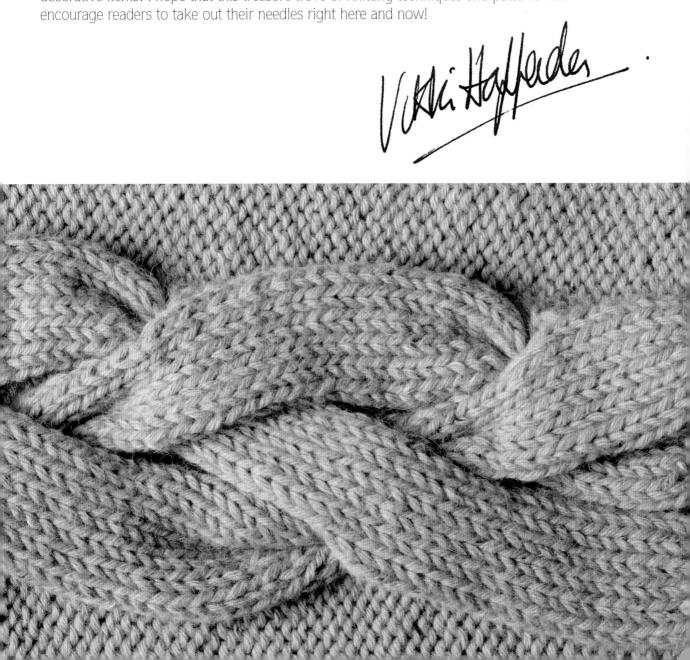

Whatever your knitting ability, the resulting items will look more professional if the appropriate techniques are worked correctly. To help with this you will find that the Techniques section provides in-depth instruction on a variety of finishing methods, edgings, and embellishments. There are a number of simpler projects included that are suitable for beginners, while those with more advanced skills may choose from the entire inspirational selection of practical and decorative items. I hope that this treasure trove of knitting techniques and patterns will encourage readers to take out their needles right here and now!

Tools and materials

Yarns

Yarn is the long, stranded, spun fiber that we knit with. There are many types of yarn, allowing knitters to enjoy a variety of sensory experiences as they express themselves through the medium. Yarn may be made of different fibers (see pp. 10–13) and have a range of textures (see pp. 14–15). The possibilities are exciting: you can, in theory, knit with anything—from a skein of supple silk sock yarn to the plastic bag that you brought it home in. Choose from a color palette that sweeps from subtle, muted tones to eye-popping brights.

Fibers

Yarns, like fabrics, are made from fibers. A fiber may be the hair from an animal, man-made (synthetics), or derived from a plant. The fibers are processed and spun to make yarn. Yarn may be made from a single fiber, such as wool, or mixed with other fibers to enhance its attributes (for example, to affect its durability or softness). Different blends are also created for aesthetic reasons, such as mixing soft, luxurious cashmere with a rougher wool. As a result, all yarns have different properties, so it is important to choose an appropriate blend for your project.

Natural fibers

← Wool

The hair, or wool, of a variety of breeds of sheep, such as the Shetland Moorit or Bluefaced Leicester, is made into pure wool yarns, or blended with other fibers. It is very warm and hard-wearing, and great for winter wear, such as jackets, cardigans, hats, and gloves. Some wool is rough, but it will soften with wear and washing. Wool sold as "organic" generally contains a higher proportion of lanolin, offering a soft but strong yarn that retains some of its natural water-repellent properties.

← Merino wool

This is wool from the merino sheep, which is said to have one of the softest wools of any sheep breed. The bouncy, smooth-surfaced fiber is just as warm as a more wiry, coarse wool. Merino is a fantastic choice for wearing against the skin, and is often treated to make it suitable for machine-washing. Good for soft scarves, arm warmers, and children's garments.

← Mohair

This fiber is the hair of the Angora goat, and it produces a unique natural "halo" when knitted up. Working with it is quite challenging, since its frizzy appearance makes it difficult to see the structure of the knitting and any mistakes made. Mohair makes particularly interesting oversized sweaters and accessories. It is not advisable to use it for baby clothes, since it may shed hair when newly made, which could be dangerous if inhaled.

← Alpaca

This fiber has a luxurious feel and is one of the warmest natural fibers you can knit with. Even a fine, sport-weight garment provides sufficient insulation in bitterly cold weather. The alpaca is related to the llama. Alpaca yarn is perfect for ski hats and thick, cozy sweaters and socks. You will also find baby alpaca yarn available, which is softer still.

← Cashmere

This fiber is the hair from a goat, which makes an ultra-luxurious, velvety soft yarn. It is light but incredibly strong, and weighs very little by the yard; it often goes further than a pure wool or cotton yarn. It is expensive to produce and is often blended with other fibers in a yarn to add softness. Cashmere can be enjoyed close to the skin in scarves, snoods, or sweaters. Treat it with great care; may be dry-clean only.

← Angora

The lush coat of the Angora rabbit produces a fiber that is softer and lighter than mohair, and produces the same furry "halo" effect. Each individual rabbit hair is very silky and long, and the resulting spun yarns, although soft, are inclined to shed slightly. Angora makes particularly pretty hats, but is very delicate and so is not recommended for bags or homewares.

← Soy or milk protein

Proteins derived from soy and milk can be used to make fibers, which are often seen in blended yarns. The stringy, sleek fibers add a soft, silky quality to rougher fibers such as linen or wool. Yarns containing soy or milk protein are less likely to be machine-washable, and do not retain heat particularly well. They are suitable for lightweight shrugs, flowing cardigans, and summer wear.

Mercerized cotton ↑

Cotton fiber can be mercerized, a treatment during which it undergoes mechanical and chemical processing to compress it and transform it into an ultra-strong yarn with a reflective sheen. It is a fine choice of fiber for a project that needs to be strong and hold its shape, such as a shiny evening bag, a long summer cardigan, or a throw.

Linen ↑

This fiber is commonly derived from the flax plant. It is rather wiry, with an oily, waxy surface, but blossoms into a sleek, soft, breathable yarn that is ideal for knitting into lightweight cardigans and tops to wear in warm weather.

Matte cotton ↑

Cotton is the fluffy mass that grows around the seeds of the cotton plant. It is spun into a breathable, summery fiber. Most cotton yarns are easy to wash and, when cared for correctly, can be incredibly robust and last for decades. It is therefore a good fiber for homewares, knitted pouches, and shoulder bags. Pure, untreated cotton is ideal for hand-dyeing.

Silk ↑

The silkworm, a caterpillar that eats mulberry leaves, spins a cocoon in order to develop into a moth. It is from the fibers of the cocoon that silk is made. Silk is shiny and sleek, very delicate and, because of its extraordinary source, very expensive. The luxurious texture of silk yarn makes it ideal for wedding and baptismal gifts, and indulgent fitted knitwear.

Synthetic fibers

← Microfiber

With a quality of velvety softness, microfiber is increasingly common in yarn blends, since it is efficient at holding other fibers together as one yarn. Synthetic fibers such as this may not appeal to you, but they are often included in a yarn to reduce density, add texture, or to prevent excess spun fiber from migrating and pilling on the surface of a piece of knitting.

← Nylon
Polyamide, or nylon, is an incredibly strong and lightweight fiber. Its elasticity makes it perfect for use in knitted fabrics, and it is often used to reinforce yarn blends for items that may be subjected to heavy wear, such as sock and darning yarns. Like other man-made fibers, nylon improves the washability of the fibers it is blended with by preventing shrinkage and felting.

Yarn blends

← Wool and cotton mixes
The strength and softness of cotton adds smoothness, breathability, and washability to wool's very warm (and sometimes scratchy) qualities. The blend is great for those with sensitive skin and babies. Cotton and wool absorb dye differently, which may lead to a stranded color appearance in such blends. Wool sheds fewer hairs when mixed with a stabilizing plant fiber.

← Natural and synthetic mixes
Man-made fibers are often blended with natural fibers to bring structure, strength, and washability; also to alter their appearance, such as to add a sheen. They help bind other yarns such as mohair and wool together and prevent shedding; they also prevent animal fibers from shrinking. The strength of such blends makes them perfect for socks or gloves.

← Synthetic-only mixes
Manufacturers can mix man-made, easily manipulated fibers to create a variety of textures, such as furry eyelash yarns, soft and smooth babywear yarns, and rough Aran substitutes. Although they do not hold much warmth in comparison to animal fibers, most synthetic-only blends can be washed at a high temperature and tumble-dried.

Specialty yarns and textural effects

For knitters who love something a bit different, specialty yarns make life very exciting. From velvety chenille to yarns with different textures, there are lots to experiment with. Each creates a different effect when knitted into a fabric, perhaps even looking like a fabric that has not been knitted at all! Read this section to bring out your inner textile artist, and let the yarns inspire you to create something fresh and edgy.

← Chenille

This yarn is often composed of cotton and synthetics and is made up of short fibers emerging from a strong core. A fabric knitted in it will have a luxurious, velvety feel. Chenille is ideal for a plain stockinette stitch, but less so for intricate patterns and for work, such as lace and cables, since it can hide the detail. It is a delicate yarn, which is likely to deteriorate with heavy wear and tear. It is therefore most suitable for plain-knitted garments for adults, and for hats and scarves.

← Plied yarn

A plied yarn is made up from more than one strand of spun fiber. Originally, the number of "plies" held together in a yarn (i.e., 4-ply, 6-ply, or 8-ply) defined its thickness. Plied yarns often have a solid, bold appearance when knitted, with a good stitch definition, allowing you to see knitted textures and patterns clearly. They often contain several colors to give a mottled, tweedy effect. The yarn is widely available in a variety of fiber mixtures and is suitable for use in most knitting projects.

← Slubby yarn

This type of yarn is often spun by hand, and is characterized by a varying thickness along its length. This mixture of thick and thin areas creates a unique, uneven, and somewhat lumpy fabric when knitted. The texture produced by slubby yarn makes unusual accessories and outerwear such as jackets.

← Braided yarn

Two or more fibers are blended together to make a braided yarn. It often has a soft fiber, such as wool or cotton, for the core, which is then wrapped in a fiber such as nylon or a metallic blend. The mixture of fibers improves stitch definition: stitches are individually highlighted by the wrapping fiber around the core yarn.

← Loose-spun yarn

This type of yarn is usually more aerated and less dense than a regular yarn, as it is more loosely spun. When knitted, it is light and bouncy, and very soft. Very thick yarns are often spun in this way to prevent knitted garments from feeling too heavy, or subsequently losing their shape when worn. These thick yarns are good for chunky, quick-to-knit accessories such as snoods and leg warmers.

← Tape yarn

The main characteristic of tape yarn is its flat shape. It may also be tubular, and is flattened when wound into a ball. A fabric knitted in it varies, depending on whether you twist the yarn when knitting, or lay it flat over the needle when working each individual stitch. Twisting it will produce a nubbly fabric; laying it flat will produce a smooth surface on the finished item.

← Bouclé yarn

The curly appearance of bouclé yarn results from whirls of fiber attached to a solid core yarn. When knitted, these loops of fiber stand out and create a carpetlike looped fabric. (Bouclé is also the name of a type of fabric manufactured using a similarly spun yarn.) Bouclé yarns are completely unique and often specify a deceptively larger gauge guideline as a result of their overall thickness. Bouclé is a lovely choice for very simply shaped garments, or for adding interest to plain stockinette-stitch knits by inserting an area using this alternative texture.

← Tweed yarn

The term "tweed" describes a classic fiber mixture in both yarns and woven cloth. Tweed is most often composed of natural wool fibers spun with intermingled flecks of contrasting colors. The first tweeds were made of undyed cream wool and undyed wool from another breed of sheep with darker hair to create a cream yarn with brown or black flecks, most recognizable in traditional Aran or fishermen's sweaters. Now, tweed yarns come in a variety of colors with an assortment of contrasting flecks, from bright to subtle, for a knit with layers of artistic interest.

Yarn labels

Everything you need to know about a yarn is on its label. It will include symbols that tell you how to knit with it and how to clean it. Here is just a selection of the most common symbols. Always keep the labels—they are vital for identifying the yarn if you run short and need more. New yarn needs to have the same dye lot number as the original purchase in order to avoid a slight difference in color in the finished item.

SYMBOLS

Yarn manufacturers may use a system of symbols to give details of a yarn. These include descriptions of suitable needles and the required gauge.

YARN WEIGHT AND THICKNESS

RECOMMENDED NEEDLE SIZE

GAUGE OVER A 4IN (10CM) TEST SQUARE

SHADE/COLOR NUMBER

DYE LOT NUMBER

WEIGHT AND LENGTH OF YARN IN BALL

FIBER CONTENT

MACHINE-WASH COLD

MACHINE-WASH COLD, GENTLE CYCLE

HAND-WASH COLD

HAND-WASH WARM

DO NOT BLEACH

DRY-CLEANABLE IN ANY SOLVENT

DRY-CLEANABLE IN CERTAIN SOLVENTS

DO NOT DRY-CLEAN

DO NOT TUMBLE-DRY

DO NOT IRON

IRON ON A LOW HEAT

IRON ON A MEDIUM HEAT

Ballband →

A yarn label is also known as a ballband. It features information on the yarn's weight and thickness as well as washing guidelines. Yarns range from the fingering and light to the thick, chucky, and bulky.

Choosing yarn colors

When embarking on a new knitting project, the choice of color is a very important decision. The color wheel is a useful tool that will introduce you to color theory. Each segment shows the hue, shade, tone, and tint of a color. A hue is the pure, bright color; a shade is the color mixed with black; a tone is the color mixed with gray; and a tint is the color mixed with white (pastels). The use of color can affect the appearance of a project dramatically. When picking colors for Fair Isle, use a mixture of dark, midtone, and pale shades to optimize the contrasts in the pattern.

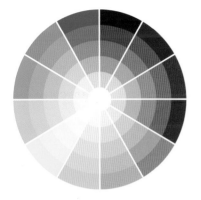

← Using a color wheel
Artists use this to see how colors work together. Blue, red, and yellow are primary colors; green, orange, and purple are secondary colors; and the colors in between these are tertiary colors. Colors that lie side by side harmonize with each other. Colors that are directly opposite, such as purple and yellow, complement each other and provide a bold contrast in a design.

Black and white Black and white are not included on the color wheel, since they are not classified as colors. Black is an absence of all color and white is a combination of all colors in the spectrum. Keep in mind that when using black, not only is your work more difficult to see, but also that complex cables and texture work will not be seen to best effect in the final garment. White, however, guarantees that every stitch and detail will be clear; the drawback is that white knits show smudges of dirt more quickly and therefore need to be washed more frequently.

← Warm shades
The warm end of the color spectrum consists mainly of red and yellow tones; browns, oranges, and purple are part of this group. Use these colors to bring richness and depth. A blend of warm shades can be a very flattering mixture to use, depending on your coloring; hold yarn against your face to see what suits you.

← Cool shades
Blue, green, and violet are at the cool end of the spectrum, and these can look very good used together. Cool colors are generally darker in tone than warm ones. If used with warm shades, their impact is lessened; if you need to balance a warm mixture in a project, you will need a higher proportion of cool to warm colors to do it.

← Pastels
These very pale, often cool variations of deeper, darker colors are very popular for babies' and small children's garments; consequently, a variety of suitable synthetic yarns and blends are available. Pastels also feature strongly in spring/summer knitting patterns for adults; look for ice-cream colors in lightweight yarns, and enjoy using a delicate color palette.

← Brights
Vivid and fluorescent shades are fun to use in a project, and often make particularly eye-catching accessories or intarsia motifs. A great way to liven up a colorwork project that consists of muted shades is to add a bright edging or set of buttons. This burst of color can change the project's overall impact completely.

Yarn weights

Yarns come in many different weights and thicknesses, which affect the appearance of a finished item and the number of stitches required to knit a sample gauge swatch of 4in (10cm). Find the most suitable weight of yarn, according to the project, below. The samples on page 19 show what the yarns look like when knitted in stockinette stitch (p. 59). The yarn weight names give the common US term(s) first, followed by the UK term(s).

YARN WEIGHT CHART

WHAT DO YOU WANT TO KNIT?	YARN WEIGHT	YARN SYMBOL	RECOMMENDED NEEDLE SIZES		
			METRIC	US	OLD UK
LACE	Fingering, lace, 2-ply	0 Fingering	2mm 2.25mm 2.5mm	0 1	14 13
FINE-KNIT SOCKS, SHAWLS, BABY CLOTHES	Sock, fingering, baby, superfine, 3-ply	1 Sock	2.75mm 3mm 3.25mm	2 N/A 3	12 11 10
LIGHT SWEATERS, BABY CLOTHES, SOCKS, ACCESSORIES	Sport, 4-ply, fine, baby	2 Sport	3.5mm 3.75mm 4mm	4 5 6	N/A 9 8
SWEATERS, LIGHT-WEIGHT SCARVES, BLANKETS, TOYS	DK, Double-knit, light worsted, 5–6 ply	3 DK	4.5mm	7	7
SWEATERS, CABLED MENSWEAR, BLANKETS, HATS, SCARVES, MITTENS	Worsted, Aran, medium, Afghan, 12-ply	4 Worsted	5mm 5.5mm	8 9	6 5
RUGS, JACKETS, BLANKETS, HATS, LEG WARMERS, WINTER ACCESSORIES	Chunky, bulky, craft, rug, 14-ply	5 Chunky	6mm 6.5mm 7mm 8mm	10 10½ N/A 11	4 3 2 0
HEAVY BLANKETS, RUGS, THICK SCARVES	Bulky, super bulky, super chunky, roving, 16-ply and upward	6 Bulky	9mm 10mm	13 15	00 000

KNITTING WITH DIFFERENT WEIGHTS OF YARN

FINGERING/LACE
Extremely light and often sold in a plentiful quantity. If worked on needles of the recommended size, the yarn produces a very fine-knit, delicate result. It can be more pleasurable to use the yarn with slightly larger needles for a more open fabric and a slightly quicker knit.

SOCK/BABY
An ideal choice for lightweight lace work. It goes a long way per ball and requires very slim needles. A gossamer yarn such as this one highlights stitch definition and very fine detail, and intricate lace work looks stunning in it.

SPORT
Many knitters prefer sport-weight to sock-weight, since it uses a more comfortable needle size yet still produces a very fine knit. This yarn is good for socks and baby clothes; the small stitches and neat appearance also suit items with designs that feature texture or colorwork.

DK (DOUBLE-KNIT)/ LIGHT WORSTED/5–6 PLY
Double-knit yarn is used for anything from blankets and toys to sweaters and cardigans. It is commonly associated with US6 (UK8/4mm) needles, and this slightly thicker alternative to 4-ply yarn knits up more quickly and may therefore be preferable to work with.

WORSTED
This thick, warm yarn commonly uses US8 (UK6/5mm) needles. It is good for men's garments with thick cabled detail, and the result is not too heavy. Good for functional items; many yarns in this thickness employ a large variety of fibers to make them machine-washable.

CHUNKY/14-PLY
Although bulky, the yarn mainly consists of lightweight fibers to prevent garments from drooping out of shape over time. Commonly worked on US10½ (UK2/7mm) needles to create a chunky fabric for outerwear, hats, and leg warmers. Quick to knit; perfect for gifts.

BULKY/16 PLY+
The yarn thickness varies, but it is commonly used with very large needles from US15 (UK000/10mm) upward. A great choice for beginners, since stitches are so large that mistakes are easily visible. Knits up very quickly; good for rugged scarves.

Knitting needles

Experienced knitters often settle on a preferred needle type according to their knitting style and gauge. Needles come in assorted types and are made of different materials, and both have benefits when using particular techniques or working with certain fibers. Discover here how to choose the most suitable needles for the project you have in mind.

Straight needles

Straight needles give a great deal of support to the hand when knitting. If you are new to knitting, start with these. Short needles are recommended for small projects; long needles are more suitable for wider knits, such as a sweater or a baby's blanket, and for knitters who like to work by holding the needles underneath their arms or elbows.

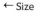

← Size
Knitting needles vary in diameter, from just 1/16 in (1.5mm) thick to over 1in (25mm). There are three common needle-sizing systems: European metric, old British sizes, and American sizes. The chart opposite shows you how to convert between systems; notice that there are not always exact equivalents. Needles are also available in various lengths to suit different projects and different ways of holding needles.

Metal needles ↑
When working with hairy fibers such as mohair or wool, which may stick, slippery metal needles are great. If you find that you tend to knit too tightly, the slippery surface can help, since it will cause a knitter's gauge to loosen. Needles of more than US11 (UK0/8mm) in diameter can be clunky to work with, so are rarely available.

Plastic needles ↑
For needles with a surface that is halfway between that of metal and that of bamboo, choose plastic. Plastic remains at a steady temperature during use, which may suit people who have arthritis. Avoid plastic needles of US6 (UK8/4mm) or smaller, since heavy projects may bend or break them.

Bamboo needles ↑
Bamboo is a lightweight, flexible material, and makes excellent knitting needles. It helps to keep stitches regularly spaced, creating an evenly knitted fabric. Great for slippery fibers such as silk, mercerized cotton, and bamboo yarn. Recommended for arthritis sufferers. Thin needles will gradually warp slightly with use to fit the curvature of your hand.

CONVERSION CHART
This chart gives the closest equivalents between the three needle-sizing systems. If you have some old needles and are not sure of their size, buy a needle size gauge (see p. 22) and push the needles through a selection of holes to establish their size.

EU METRIC	OLD UK	US
1.5mm	N/A	000 00
2mm	14	0
2.25mm 2.5mm	13	1
2.75mm	12	2
3mm	11	N/A
3.25mm	10	3
3.5mm	N/A	4
3.75mm	9	5
4mm	8	6
4.5mm	7	7
5mm	6	8
5.5mm	5	9
6mm	4	10
6.5mm	3	10½
7mm	2	N/A
7.5mm	1	N/A
8mm	0	11
9mm	00	13
10mm	000	15
12mm	N/A	17
15mm	N/A	19
20mm	N/A	35
25mm	N/A	50

Ebony/rosewood needles ↑

These wooden needles feel luxurious to work with, and can be quite expensive. They often have a waxy surface, which becomes smooth with wear, creating a soft and tactile surface. Like bamboo needles, they help to create an even fabric; they hold their shape and remain straight when used, giving them a solid feel.

Square needles ↓

Most needles are cylindrical with a pointed tip; these unusual new needles have a faceted surface and a pointed tip. Made from metal, they lie over each other better, which is particularly useful when working with double-pointed needles, and cause less strain on the hands, making them especially suitable for arthritis sufferers.

Double-pointed and circular needles

Some projects require you to knit in the round, to produce a tube of knitting without a seam. You can use both double-pointed needles and circular needles to do this, but the choice of needles is usually down to length. Most circular needles are too large to knit socks or gloves on, so double-pointed needles, which can knit a very narrow tube, are used instead. Your gauge and style will change according to which you use.

Bamboo double-pointed needles

Metal double-pointed needles

Plastic double-pointed needles

← **Double-pointed needles**

The recommended option for socks and gloves, and narrow tubes. These needles are short and do not accommodate a large number of stitches. At first, some knitters may find that ladders form on each corner between the needles; however, this problem will disappear over time as you practice. Double-pointed needles are less slippery when made of bamboo or wood and most people agree that these types are more comfortable to work with.

Circular needles ↑

A flexible tube joins two needles to make a pair of circular needles. These come in a selection of different lengths and thicknesses. It is important to choose a length that is most appropriate for your project: it should match the anticipated diameter of the knitted tube. For instance, a hat would call for shorter circular needles than a sweater knitted in this way. Knitting patterns usually specify the size and length required. A piece of flat knitting can also be worked on circular needles: just turn your needles around after each row instead of working in the round.

Interchangeable circular needles ↑

These are a worthwhile investment if you think you will use circular needles frequently in the future, or if you generally prefer to use circular knitting needles for all your knitting projects. The set comes with connecting tubes or wires in various lengths, and a selection of tips. Simply attach your chosen tips to each end of the wire to "build" a pair of circular needles to a specific length and size. Some sets allow you to attach several wires together to create very long circular needles.

Other equipment

Hundreds of different gadgets are available for knitters. Some are merely for convenience, whereas others are absolutely vital and perform specific tasks. Here are the absolute essentials; the more advanced, specialized items are shown on pp. 24–25.

The essentials

These basic items should always be on hand when you are working on a project. Most knitters have a portable knitting bag or case to keep them in, so that it is easy to take everything to wherever they want to sit and knit. The tools below are relatively inexpensive and can be purchased from craft stores and yarn shops.

← Knitting needle gauge
Many knitting needles, such as double-pointed needles, circular needles, interchangeable needles, and vintage needles are not marked with a size. It is vital to know what size a needle is, so poke it through the holes in the gauge to find out. Many also feature a ruler, which you can use to measure gauge swatches.

Scissors ↓
Keep a pair of good-quality scissors on hand for cutting off yarn and trimming ends. Sharp, short-bladed scissors are perfect: They allow you to snip very close to the work and so trim darned-in ends neatly when finishing a seam.

← Pins
The large head on these pins prevents them from getting lost in a piece of work. Use them to pin pieces of knitting together when finishing work, as well as to pin out work to the correct measurements when blocking.

Stitch holders →
These are used to hold stitches that you will return to later. You could make your own stitch holder from a length of lightweight cotton yarn, a safety pin, or a paper clip.

Tape measure ↑
Use this to measure the person you are knitting for, and for gauging sizing accurately. Also use it to check gauge and measure knitting. Stick to either standard or metric measurements, but not a mixture of both.

← Stitch markers
Use these to mark the beginning and end of a panel of stitches, and to identify the end of each row when working in the round. As you arrive at a marker, transfer it from the right-hand to the left-hand needle; continue working the row as normal.

Needle organizer ↑
Use this to keep your knitting needles organized and protected against damage. Needle rolls and bags are available in a range of shapes and sizes. Thick needles are best suited to a needle bag (like a long pencil case); double-pointed needles can be stored in a short needle roll.

← Row counter
Available as a tube that sits at the end of a knitting needle: change the counter when you complete a row; also as a clicker, which you "click" each time you finish a row.

Knitting bag ↓
Bags for knitters often have many compartments, perfect for storing equipment and materials for your current project. To protect knitting from damp and moths, keep a cedar cube (see p. 28) inside.

Point protectors ↑
Place these over fragile needle tips to guard against damage; use them to protect your knitting bag from punctures; and to stop stitches from sliding off needles and unraveling when not in use.

Specialized equipment

As you begin to use more advanced techniques, you will find that you need specialized equipment. Each item is specific to a particular skill, such as colorwork, lace knitting, and patterning with cables. If you are a new knitter and just learning the basic stitches, you won't need these items, but you will certainly need them in the future as you become more experienced and try more ambitious projects.

← Sharp-ended needles
Buy these with a large eye; use to secure darned-in ends after finishing with the blunt-ended needle. A sharp needle may also be required when inserting a zipper or affixing trimmings to a piece of work.

Blunt-ended yarn needles ↑
To sew up projects and darn in ends, you need a selection of blunt-ended yarn needles. These will not damage or split delicate fibers when penetrating knitting to sew a seam, instead, nudging them out of the way. Some have a curved tip, which will speed up the sewing-up process by resurfacing along your seam more quickly than a straight needle.

← Crochet hook
Available in different materials such as metal, wood, and bamboo. A crochet hook makes it much easier to pick up dropped stitches. The slippery surface of the metal version probably makes this the most user-friendly type. You can also use a crochet hook for inserting tassels.

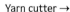

Tapestry needles ↑
These have a blunt tip in order to prevent damage to fibers, so are also suitable for use by knitters. Make sure that the eye is an appropriate size for the yarn; do not force yarn through an eye that is too small or it will split it.

Yarn cutter →
A convenient alternative to scissors. Insert the yarn through the grooves in the yarn cutter in order to trim it off. You may prefer to attach it to a cord to wear around your neck while you work.

↑ Blocking wire and pins
These are used to block lace work. Thread the wire through the edge of the work, as though making a long running stitch. The wire stays in the knitting and supports it; it remains flexible after hand-washing the item, so the work can be reshaped and dried flat.

← Sock blocker
This is the best way to block finished socks to a neat shape. Hand-wash the sock and pull gently to shape on the blocker. As it dries, it will take on the shape of the blocker. Sock blockers are available in a selection of sizes. If you use a wooden version, the sock can be lightly steamed to shape instead.

Cable needle ↑
A kinked or U-shaped cable needle is used when working cables; this shape prevents cable stitches from sliding away. Choose a size that is closest to that of the needles used for the main body of the knitting.

Yarn bobbins ↑

In the intarsia method of colorwork, you create numerous lengths of yarn in different colors in order to work separate parts of each knitted row. These handy bobbins keep each color neatly wound as you work.

← Swift

Use a swift together with a ball-winder to transform a hank or skein of yarn into convenient balls in double-quick time. Lay the yarn around the edges of the swift and attach it to the ball-winder. If you don't have a swift, you will need to find a volunteer to hold the yarn, or place it on a chair back as you use the ball-winder.

Chart paper →

Use knitters' graph paper for recording a colorwork design or making a pattern chart. Knitted stitches are not square: they are wider than they are tall, so standard graph paper will not be suitable. Buy ready-printed chart paper from a craft store, or download free from the Internet.

Pom-pom rings ↑

If you want to make a pom-pom to trim a hat, try these reusable circular plastic templates. Wind the yarn around the template, snip around the edge, and secure with a strand of yarn to draw it all together. You could also make your own out of cardboard, or use a pom-pom machine to make one quickly by winding a handle.

← Ball-winder

This device allows you to wind hanks of yarn into balls quickly, instead of doing it by hand. Alternatively, use this handy tool to wind two or more strands together before you knit them, to make an evenly spun, double-stranded yarn.

← Sock keepers

In a similar way to point protectors for regular needles, these sock keepers are used to prevent stitches from falling off double-pointed needles when they are not in use.

← Knitting dolly/I-cord-maker

An I-cord is a narrow tube of knitting. The best way to make one is to use a knitting dolly. Alternatively, a mechanical I-cord-maker, suitable for DK-weight yarns, allows you to make long I-cords much more quickly. There are larger versions for thicker yarns, which produce chunkier I-cords.

Other equipment

Embellishments

Add dazzle and give your knitting an edge by adding embellishments, from embroidery to beads, sequins, pretty trimmings, clever fastenings, and attractive notions such as handles. These can completely change the feel of a project, depending on the way that you use them. Embellishment gives you an opportunity to express your creativity: try some of the ideas here.

← Embroidery thread

Silky, shiny embroidery threads come in a mixture of colors and styles. Metallic threads are particularly interesting and will jazz up a solid knitted background. Use a tapestry needle to embroider knitting, remembering that most embroidery threads stipulate that they must be hand-washed.

Machine embroidery thread →

This thread is very fine and is sold on cones or small spools. It is intended for machine embroidery, but you could try double-stranding a metallic one (check its yardage) with a knitting yarn for a subtle hint of sparkle. Alternatively, use variegated threads, or several at the same time, with the yarn.

Knitting beads ↑

Most knitting beads are specially manufactured to be washable, and retain their color over time, whereas other types may not withstand wear and washing. They come in different sizes for specific thicknesses of yarn, such as 4-ply, for example.

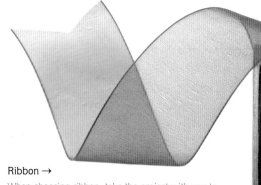

Ribbon →

When choosing ribbon, take the project with you to color-coordinate effectively (although you may feel able to remember a color, this is unreliable). Among the vast choice available, you could try organza, patterned, striped, or metallic ribbons. Thread them through your work, trim an edge, or form them into bows or rosettes.

Trimmings ↑

There is a whole world of trimmings for dressmaking: although these are less commonly used in knitting, they can impart a frilly, delicate feel to an otherwise blocky project. Trimmings come in all shapes and sizes, from the glittery to simple broderie anglaise, as well as fringe and marabou feathers, to name but a few. Each can add an exciting dimension to your work.

Bag handles ↑

Knitted bags are given added strength when carried on solid bag handles. These will take the weight of the bag's contents without stretching out of shape or breaking. There are jazzy colored-plastic handles, wood, or metal versions available, which can be used to make a bag look classic, contemporary, or quirky.

Fastenings →

Choose fastenings with care, according to the type of project and the yarn you are using, and make sure they are not so heavy that they will pull the knitting out of shape. Buttons usually double as a feature, but other fastenings are more discreet, such as a hook and eye or a press stud. Stitch these on with knitting yarn or sewing thread. Use push-on press studs for felted work.

Sequins ↑

Knit sequins into your work as you go, or embroider them on afterward. If you're going to knit them in, look for pailettes, which have a larger hole than regular sequins, which are only suited to fine yarns. Choose flat sequins, which will sit flat against the work and each other, and are less inclined to get scratched and lose surface color.

← Buttons

The choice of buttons for a garment is an important one. They are decorative as well as serving a practical purpose; make sure you select them to suit the way that the garment will be cleaned, or they may have to be removed beforehand. Coconut, shell, wooden, and metallic buttons are fairly neutral and work with many colors. Take your project to the store to assess the way that button shapes, colors, and sizes work with it.

Garment care

After all the hard work of knitting a garment, it is important to protect it from damage and to keep it looking new. Moths are one of the biggest threats; they love to lay their eggs in natural fibers and the larvae will chew tiny holes, which are unsightly and cause knitting to fall apart. The equipment below will help you to keep your hand-knits in good condition.

← Lavender sachets
Lavender is a traditional and natural deterrent to moths. Make your own sachets from dried garden lavender, crumbled into fabric or knitted bags. Hang sachets in the closet, or slip into drawers. Use also in sealed bags of yarn for storage.

Pill remover →
Knitted items may pill (form bumps on the surface). If this is severe, shave them off with a pill-removing comb or machine. Be gentle: Do not pull at your work, since it may damage it. Fabric softeners may aggravate the problem.

Cedar rings or cubes ↑
An alternative moth deterrent, cedar wood has a subtle aroma, which some people may prefer to that of lavender. Available as cubes, blocks, and rings to hang in the closet, or to dot around a storage closet, or put inside bags or boxes of yarn. The aroma fades over time, but they can be sanded down to refresh the natural smell. Alternatively, apply a drop of grapefruit oil to each block, allow it to dry, and return the blocks to your yarn stash for a moth deterrent with added antibacterial properties.

Garment bag →
These are a must-have and are available in a variety of styles, ranging from simple zipped bags to lavender-scented plastic bags, and bags that allow vacuum packing in order to reduce bulk and save space. Make sure that bags are sealed properly to prevent damp and insects from getting in. Although a bag may appear secure when folded over, moths are able to wriggle in and out of small spaces and make themselves at home.

← Wool wash
This very gentle soap will cleanse fibers and remove dirt without damaging a yarn or leaching dye from it. It is now possible to buy a wool wash that does not need to be rinsed out, making the hand-washing of precious knitted items even more convenient.

← Mothballs
A chemical method of deterring moths and insects. Slip them into pockets or garment bags. They vary from strong-smelling to subtle; beware of the strong ones, since the smell can be impossible to eradicate.

Mohair brush →
Mohair can flatten and lose its auralike furriness after washing or prolonged storage. It is therefore essential to invest in a mohair brush to reinvigorate fuzzy knits with gentle brushstrokes. You can also prevent matting in areas subject to extra wear, such as the underarms of a sweater.

Garment care **29**

Techniques

Key techniques

Learning to knit is a very quick process. There are only a few key techniques to pick up before you are ready to make simple shapes like scarves, baby blankets, pillow covers, and throws. The basics include casting stitches onto the needle, the knit and purl stitches, and casting (or binding) off the stitches.

Making a slip knot

Before you start knitting, you must first learn how to place the first loop on the needle. This loop is called the slip knot and it is the first stitch formed when casting on stitches.

1 Begin by crossing the yarn coming from the ball over the yarn end (called the yarn tail) to form a circle.

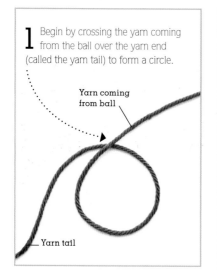

Yarn coming from ball

Yarn tail

2 Insert the tip of a knitting needle through the circle of yarn, then wrap the needle tip around the ball end of the yarn and pull the yarn through the circle.

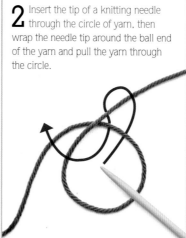

3 This forms a loop on the needle and a loose, open knot below the loop.

4 Pull both ends of the yarn firmly to tighten the knot and the loop on the needle.

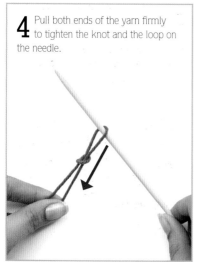

5 Make sure the completed slip knot is tight enough on the needle that it won't fall off, but not so tight that you can't slide it along.

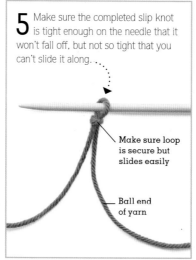

Make sure loop is secure but slides easily

Ball end of yarn

6 The yarn tail should be at least 4–6in (10–15cm) long so it can be darned in later. Your knitting pattern, however, may instruct you to leave an extra-long yarn tail (called a long loose end) to use for seams or other purposes.

Extra-long yarn tail

Holding yarn and needles

Although all knitting is formed in exactly the same way, you can hold the yarn in either the right or left hand. These two yarn-holding techniques are called the "English" and "Continental" methods. Knitting is ambidextrous, so right-handed and left-handed knitters should try both knitting styles to see which one is easier for them.

KNITTING "ENGLISH" STYLE

1 The yarn is laced around the fingers of the right hand. Aim to control the yarn firmly but with a relaxed hand, releasing it to flow through the fingers as the stitches are formed.

2 Try this alternative technique as well or make up your own. You need to hold the yarn just taut enough between your fingers to create even loops that are neither too loose nor too tight.

3 Hold the needles with the stitches about to be worked in the left hand and the other needle in the right hand. Use the right forefinger to wrap the yarn around the needle.

KNITTING "CONTINENTAL" STYLE

1 Lace the yarn through the fingers of the left hand in any way that feels comfortable. Try both to release and tension the yarn easily to create uniform loops.

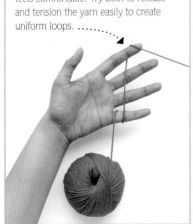

2 In this alternative technique, the yarn is wrapped twice around the forefinger.

3 Hold the needle with the unworked stitches in the left hand and the other needle in the right hand. Position the yarn with the left forefinger and pull it through the loops with the tip of the right needle.

Alternative "Continental" style knitting

This alternative method makes knit stitches very easy, and is ideal for garter or circular stockinette stitch. As you work near the tip, short tapered needles are best for this method. When knitting Continental style you may find your gauge loosens, in which case use smaller needles.

For both the knit and the purl stitches, wrap the yarn around your left little finger, but keep it over all your fingers. This makes purling easier.

ALTERNATIVE "CONTINENTAL" KNIT STITCH

1 Hold your index finger up with the yarn over it and use the pad of your middle finger to hold the yarn against the left needle, slightly forward of the stitch.

2 Insert the right tip into the stitch, pull and catch the yarn on your middle finger, draw it through the stitch on the left needle and off.

3 At the end of the row, keep the yarn around your left fingers. Swap the needles to start the next row.

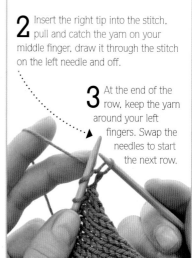

ALTERNATIVE "CONTINENTAL" PURL STITCH

1 Hold the yarn as for knit stitch. Bring yarn to front. With your index finger raised and your middle finger touching the left needle near the tip, insert needle as for purl. Tilt the right tip toward you and then back in a small circular movement so that the yarn wraps over it.

2 At the same time, bring your left index finger with the yarn on it forward, wrapping the yarn around the needle. Keep your index finger in constant contact with the left needle.

3 Immediately dip the right needle tip slightly away from you to hook the yarn and pull the old stitch open. Take the needle backward through the old stitch and make a new purl loop. Slide the old stitch off the left needle.

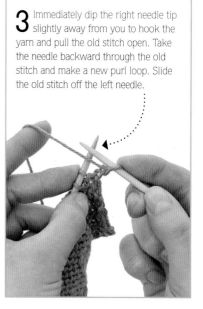

ALTERNATIVE "CONTINENTAL" PURL STITCH—UNTWISTING AN INCORRECT STITCH

1 If the front "leg" of the stitch is farther back along the needle than the rear "leg" the stitch is twisted. .....

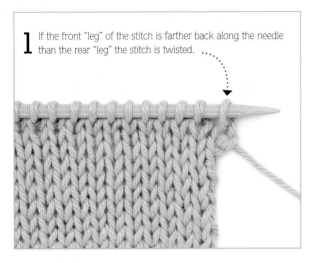

2 To untwist the stitches on the following row, knit into the back of the stitch. If you find it difficult to master the correct wrap, but still wish to purl in the Continental style, then work every knit row following a purl row by working into the back of the stitch. ....

Single strand cast-ons

These cast-ons are all related to the backward loop cast-on and use one strand. They tend to be soft, but can be made firmer by twisting. Alternating loop cast-on makes a decorative edge. Casting on knitwise and cable cast-on are useful for casting on in the middle of a piece, for example, if you need to add more than one stitch when increasing. When followed by stockinette stitch (see p. 59), casting on knitwise can curl toward the knit side. For edges where this matters, choose a two strand tubular cast-on (see p. 46).

BACKWARD LOOP CAST-ON (also called *thumb* or *single cast-on*)

1 This is the easiest cast-on. Hold the needle with the slip knot in the right hand. Then wrap the yarn around the left thumb as shown and hold the yarn in place in the palm of the left hand. Insert the needle tip under and up through the loop on the thumb following the arrow.

Yarn going to ball

Yarn tail

2 Release the loop from the thumb and pull the yarn to tighten the new cast-on loop on the needle, sliding it up close to the slip knot.

3 Loop the yarn around the thumb again and continue making loops in the same way until the required number of stitches is on the needle.

Yarn going to ball

Yarn tail

KNIT-ON CAST-ON (also called *knit-stitch cast-on*)

1 Holding the yarn in the left or right hand as explained on p. 33, place the needle with the slip knot in the left hand. Then insert the tip of the right needle from left to right through the center of the loop on the left needle.

Yarn going to ball

Long yarn tail

2 With the yarn behind the needles, wrap it under and around the tip of the right needle. (While casting on, use the left forefinger or middle finger to hold the loops on the left needle in position.)

3 With the tip of the right needle, carefully draw the yarn through the loop on the left needle. (This is the same way a knit stitch is formed, hence the name of the cast-on.)

4 Transfer the loop on the right needle to the left needle by inserting the tip of the left needle from right to left through the front of the loop.

5 Pull both yarn ends to tighten the new cast-on loop on the needle, sliding it up close to the slip knot.

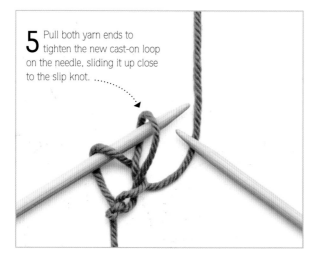

6 Continue casting on stitches in the same way until you have the required number of stitches. For a looser cast-on, hold two needles together in your left hand while casting on.

Yarn tail   Yarn going to ball

CABLE CAST-ON

1 Begin by working steps 1–5 of the knit-on cast-on (opposite). Then insert the tip of the right needle between the two loops on the left needle and wrap the yarn under and around the tip of the right needle.

Yarn going to ball

Long yarn tail

2 With the tip of the right needle, draw the yarn through to form a loop on the right needle.

3 Transfer the loop on the right needle to the left needle (see step 4 opposite). Continue, inserting the needle between the first two loops on the left needle when beginning each new cast-on stitch.

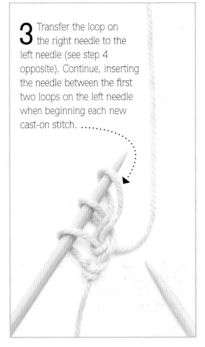

FINGER LOOP CAST-ON

1 This gives a soft cast-on. Hold the needle with the slip knot in the right hand. Lift the yarn from underneath with your left index finger pointing away from you. Bend and turn your finger to point toward you.

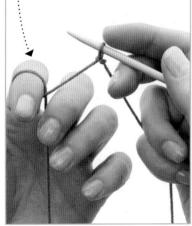

2 Insert the needle into the loop that lies on top of the finger from behind.

3 Release the index finger and tighten the stitch on the needle.

ALTERNATING LOOP CAST-ON

1 Work the first stitch as for finger loop cast-on, as shown on p. 37.

2 Work the second stitch as backward loop cast-on: lift the yarn from behind with the left thumb, wind it around the thumb, and insert the needle into the front strand (see p. 35).

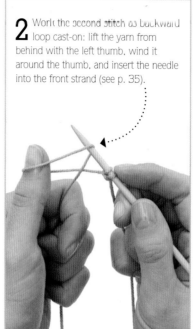

3 Repeat steps 1 and 2 to cast on as many stitches as you need. On the first row, work into the front of the stitches, even if they look twisted.

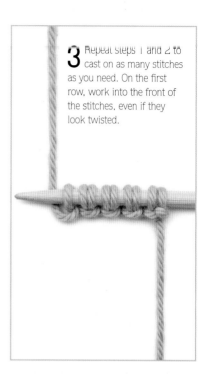

DOUBLE TWIST LOOP CAST-ON

This is firmer than backward loop cast-on, and the first row is a little easier to knit.

1 Hold the needle with the slip knot in your right hand. Lift the yarn from behind with your left index finger.

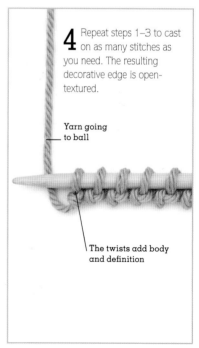

2 Twist the yarn by twirling your finger twice in a counterclockwise circle.

3 Place the loop from your finger on the needle and pull to tighten.

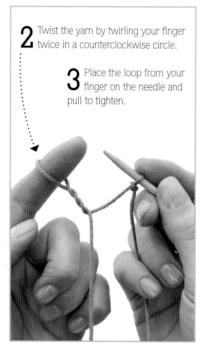

4 Repeat steps 1–3 to cast on as many stitches as you need. The resulting decorative edge is open-textured.

Yarn going to ball

The twists add body and definition

Two strand cast-on

These cast-on techniques all use two strands, but generally only one needle, and are strong, elastic, and versatile. They are usually followed by a wrong side row, unless the reverse is the right side. As with long-tail cast-on, start all these with a slip knot made after a long tail at least three times as long as the planned knitting width.

LONG-TAIL CAST-ON (also called *double cast-on*)

1 Make a slip knot on the needle, leaving a very long yarn tail—allow about 1⅜in (3.5cm) for each stitch being cast on. Hold the needle in your right hand. Then loop the yarn tail over the left thumb and the ball yarn end over the left forefinger as shown. Hold both strands in the palm of the left hand.

Long yarn tail

Yarn going to ball

2 Insert the tip of the needle under and up through the loop on the thumb.

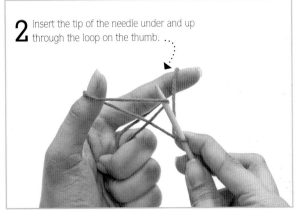

3 Wrap the tip of the needle around the loop on the forefinger from right to left and use it to pull the yarn through the loop on the thumb as shown by the arrow.

4 Release the loop from the thumb.

5 Pull both yarn ends to tighten the new cast-on loop on the needle, sliding it up close to the slip knot.

6 Loop the yarn around the thumb again and cast on another stitch in the same way. Make as many stitches as you need.

Yarn going to ball

Yarn tail

CONTRAST EDGE CAST-ON

1 Cut a piece of contrast yarn three times the length of the cast-on, and tie one end onto the end of the ball of main colored yarn.

2 Hold both strands of yarn in your left hand, with the contrast yarn toward you and the knot at the end.

3 Slide the needle along between the yarns so that the knot sits snugly on the right side of the needle. Hold it in place with your right index finger. ⋯⋯⋯⋯⋯

Main yarn

Contrast yarn

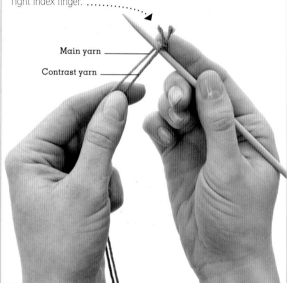

4 Loop the contrast yarn over your thumb by moving it in a counterclockwise circle, and loop the main color over your index finger as shown. ⋯⋯⋯⋯

5 Insert the needle from below under the front strand of the contrast yarn on the thumb.

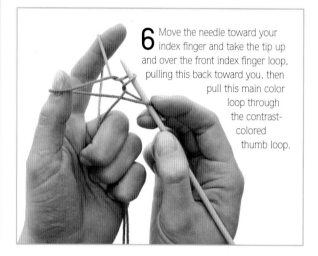

6 Move the needle toward your index finger and take the tip up and over the front index finger loop, pulling this back toward you, then pull this main color loop through the contrast-colored thumb loop.

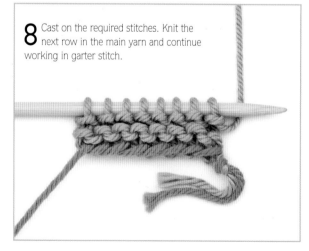

7 Release the contrast yarn thumb loop. Pull both yarn ends to hold the needle snugly, and slide the cast-on stitch close to the slip knot. Repeat steps 4—7. ⋯

8 Cast on the required stitches. Knit the next row in the main yarn and continue working in garter stitch.

TWISTED LONG-TAIL CAST-ON

This cast-on is very stretchy, so is useful before a rib. It can be made even stretchier by working it over two needles held together.

1 Hold the yarn and needle as for long-tail cast-on (see p.39). Bring the needle toward you and then back under both thumb loops. ......

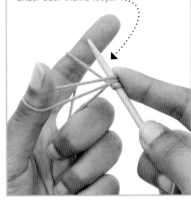

2 Bring the needle toward you over the top of the farthest thumb loop and down between both thumb strands. The thumb loop is now a figure-eight.

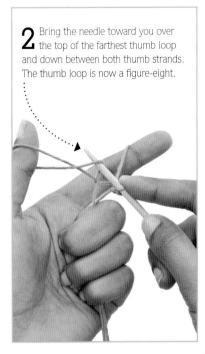

3 Take the needle over the first loop on your index finger.

4 Bring the needle toward you. Drop the end of your thumb away from you and let the loop slide down toward the end to open the thumb loop. Bring the needle down through the open thumb loop. ....

5 Release the thumb loop, keeping the yarn around your index finger ready to start the next cast-on loop. Pull the short strand to tighten the stitch.

6 Loop yarn around your thumb again and repeat steps 1–4 to cast on another stitch in the same way. The stitches create a stretchy double-twist effect.

ITALIAN CAST-ON

1 Hold the needle with the slip knot and ball yarn and in the right hand, tail in the left.

2 Bring the left index finger and thumb forward under the short yarn tail. Take the needle over and back under this strand, making a loop on the index finger.

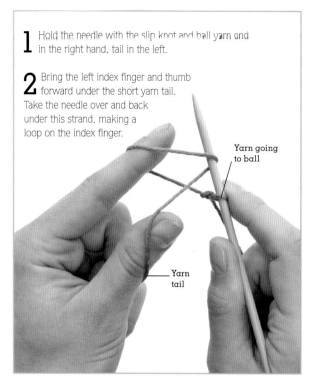

Yarn going to ball

Yarn tail

3 Holding this position, wrap the ball yarn around the needle from left to right.

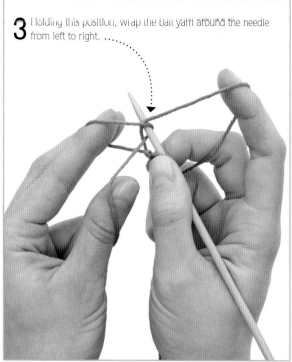

4 Slip the index finger loop over the tip of the needle. Pull the short yarn tail to tighten.

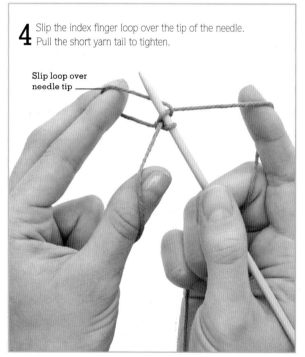

Slip loop over needle tip

5 Loop the yarn over the index finger and thumb again and continue making loops in the same way until the required number of stitches is on the needle.

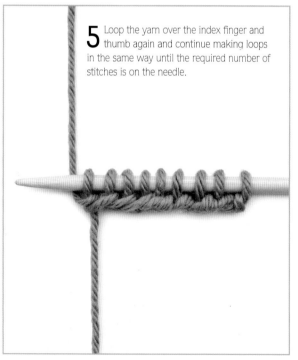

TWO-NEEDLE CAST-ON

1 Hold the needle with the slip knot in the left hand, with the short yarn tail at the back.

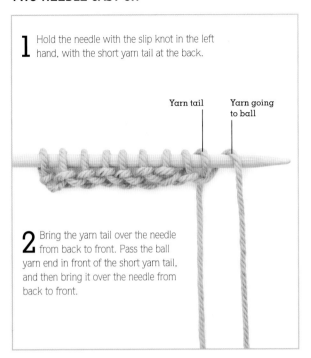

Yarn tail   Yarn going to ball

2 Bring the yarn tail over the needle from back to front. Pass the ball yarn end in front of the short yarn tail, and then bring it over the needle from back to front.

3 Using an empty needle in the right hand, pass the first loop over the second and remove the right needle.

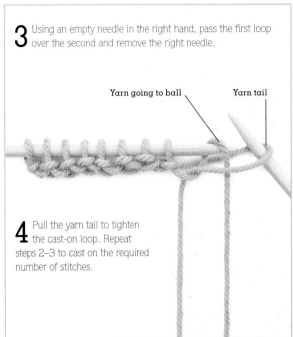

Yarn going to ball   Yarn tail

4 Pull the yarn tail to tighten the cast-on loop. Repeat steps 2–3 to cast on the required number of stitches.

TWO-STRAND LONG-TAIL CAST-ON

1 Make the first stitch as for long-tail cast-on (see p. 39). The second stitch is similar, except you turn your thumb in the opposite direction to catch the yarn. The end of the strand is now to the inside of your thumb.

2 With the needle pointing away, take it over the first thumb loop and then under the loop on the inside of the thumb. Take the needle over the nearest loop on the index finger.

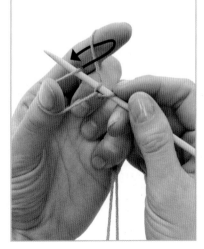

3 Draw the loop through the thumb loop.

4 Drop the thumb loop. Pull the yarn tail to tighten the new loop. Repeat to cast on the required stitches.

Special cast-ons

The following cast-ons are useful for specific purposes and may be specified in your pattern. However, many patterns simply say "cast on," in which case you should select one of these methods to add functionality or individuality to your project.

CHANNEL ISLANDS CAST-ON FOR SINGLE RIB

1 Fold the yarn tail, so that you have a doubled yarn four times the length of your cast-on edge, plus 4in (10cm).

2 Make a slip knot on the doubled strand, about 4in (10cm) down from the free end. Transfer to a needle. Hold the doubled strand in the left hand, single strand and needle in the right.

3 Bring the left thumb under the doubled strand from the front, in a clockwise circle, winding the doubled yarn twice around the thumb. Insert the needle up through both loops.

4 Pass the single strand around the needle and slip thumb loops over to make a stitch as normal.

5 Release the loop from the thumb and pull the double strand first to tighten the loop on the needle.

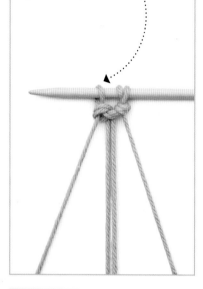

6 To make the next stitch, take the single yarn over the needle to the back (yo).

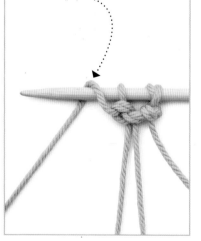

7 Repeat steps 2–4 to the required cast-on length, finishing with a thumb wrapped stitch, making an even number of stitches.

8 To work the first row, knit the first stitch (thumb loop) and purl the next (yo). Finally, purl into the initial double strand slip knot.

44   Techniques

PROVISIONAL CAST-ON

1 Take contrast yarn over twice the length of your cast-on (or a wire from a circular needle); tie a slip knot; transfer to a needle.

2 Make a slip knot in the main yarn. Transfer to the same needle.

3 Hold as for long-tail cast-on (see p. 39), with contrast yarn around the thumb.

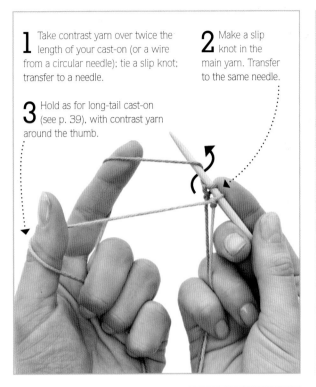

4 Flick your right wrist and take the needle down between the yarns and up under main yarn.

5 Turn the needle toward you and bring it over, and then back away from you under the contrast yarn.

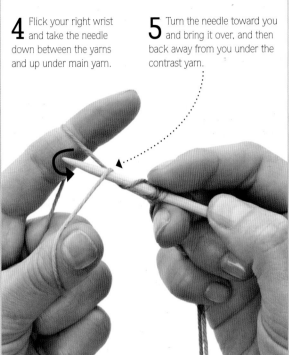

6 Catch the main yarn from above and behind, and bring it under the contrast yarn and around the needle. Let the contrast yarn slip to the back of the needle. Repeat steps 4–6 to cast on the required stitches.

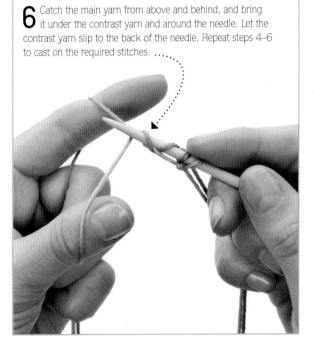

7 Drop the contrast slip knot at the end of the cast-on. Tie the contrast ends together until you want to pull the contrast yarn out and pick up the "live" open stitches. Knit into the front of the first row.

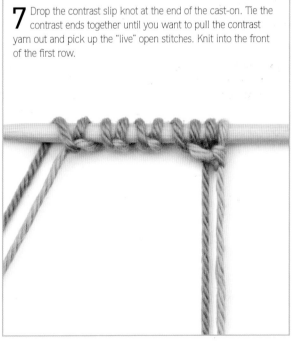

CROCHET PROVISIONAL CAST-ON

1 Make a slip knot on a crochet hook with contrast yarn. Hold yarn and needle in the left hand and hook in the right. Take the yarn behind the needle and over left index finger. Hold needle and hook crossed, with the hook in front. Lay yarn in the hook with left index finger. .....

2 Pull the yarn through the slip knot. The yarn will loop over the needle making a stitch. Take the yarn behind the needle and make another loop. Continue to cast on required stitches. Cut the yarn and pull it through the last chain on the hook. Mark this end so it is clear which end will unravel.

3 Work your knitting. ..... When ready to work on the cast-on edge, pull the marked yarn back out of the last chain after which the whole chain can be unraveled and the "live" open stitches picked up.

TUBULAR CAST-ON (also called *invisible cast-on*)

This is good for single rib, but can become wavy if overstretched. Use needles at least two sizes smaller than those used for the main fabric.

1 Hold yarn and needles as for long-tail cast-on (see p. 39), but with the palm facing down, creating a "V" of yarn pointing to the right.

2 Bring the needle forward, passing over and back under the thumb strand.

3 Catch the index-finger strand, going over and back toward you.

4 Turn your thumb away from you in a circular movement, flicking the thumb strand over the needle. Bring the left hand back to its original position, passing the yarn under the needle.

5 Make sure that the stitch goes all the way around the needle, and lies centrally under the needle.

6 Take the needle back over and under the index finger strand. With needle toward you, take it over and back under the thumb strand.

7 Move your index finger toward you in a circular movement, passing the yarn over the needle, and return your hand to its original position, making sure the stitch goes all the way around the needle. Repeat steps 2—7 to cast on an even number of stitches.

The stitches must lie under the needle

8 At the end, tie the two strands together under the needle. Knit the first row by knitting into the back of the first stitch, bring the yarn to front and slip the next stitch purlwise. Repeat along the row. For the second row, repeat without knitting into back of stitch.

ALTERNATIVE ROLL-EDGE TUBULAR CAST-ON

1 Using a smooth yarn, work a crochet provisional cast-on (see opposite) of half the required stitches plus one. In main color and on small-sized needles, knit three rows of stockinette stitch, starting with a knit row and ending with the wrong side facing.

2 Purl one stitch and take yarn to back. Insert the right needle tip from top to bottom through the purl bar of main color bar at the color join three rows down.

3 Insert the left needle from front to back into the picked-up stitch. Knit into front of stitch. Bring yarn to front. Repeat steps 2 and 3 until row is complete. Finish with a purl stitch, and no pick up.

4 Change to main needles. This cast-on makes an odd number of stitches. A single rib will have a knit stitch at each end and must be worked with rows starting as follows: knit one, purl one; then the next row purl one, knit one; and so on. Decrease one at the end of ribbing or when convenient. Remove crochet provisional cast-on.

KNOTTED CAST-ON

This can be tight, so work loosely on thick needles. This makes a strong, decorative edge.

1 Make a slip knot on the needle and cast on one stitch as long-tail cast-on (see p. 39).

2 Hold the second needle in the left hand, insert it into the slip knot and pass this over the last stitch made and off the right needle.

3 Repeat, casting on two stitches and passing first over second to required length of cast-on. Backward loop cast-on may be substituted for long-tail cast-on, if preferred. The first stitch of the first row should always be knitted.

Be sure to keep the gauge even

TWICE-KNITTED CAST-ON

Excellent for fringed edges and before twice knitted work. Always knit first stitch of first row.

1 Working loosely, make a slip knot and cast on one stitch, using the knit-on method (see p. 36).

2 Insert the right needle into both loops and knit together, but do not slip stitches off. Slip new loop from right needle to left. Knit new stitch together with the preceding stitch. Repeat step 2 to cast on required stitches.

FRILLY CAST-ON

1 Cast on an even number of stitches that is twice as many as required using the long-tail cast-on method (see p. 39). Other decorative cast-ons may be preferred.

2 Insert the right needle into the first two stitches from front to back and knit them together. Repeat across the row.

3 Work the next row as normal.

4 This creates a pretty, decorative edge. You may need extra yarn, since the cast-on uses twice as many stitches.

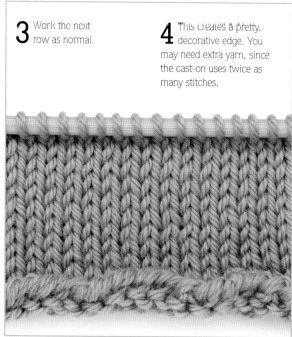

PICKED-UP EDGE CAST-ON

1 Knit a piece of a narrow edging to the required length of your cast-on. If you are unsure of the correct length, slip stitches onto a holder at the end of the row (see p. 50) and alter as necessary.

2 Work along the right side. I hold the new yarn at the back. Insert the needle tip from front to back through the first edge stitch, wrap the yarn around the needle, and pull a loop through to the front.

New yarn tail

3 Continue along the full length of the edge, picking up the new yarn evenly to form stitches on the needle. If necessary, skip some rows to prevent the cast-on from distorting.

4 Knit the main fabric upward from the edge trim as required. Start with a purl row if the main fabric is stockinette stitch.

PINHOLE CAST-ON

This is ideal for starting circular medallions.

1 Wrap the yarn around your left index finger. Insert a crochet hook, and draw a loop through as if making a slip knot. .....

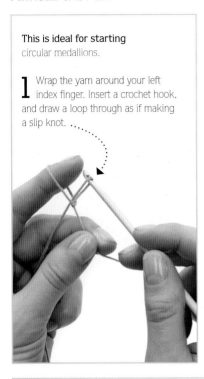

2 Keep your index finger in the knot. Hook the yarn again and draw the new loop through the loop on the hook. One stitch made. .....

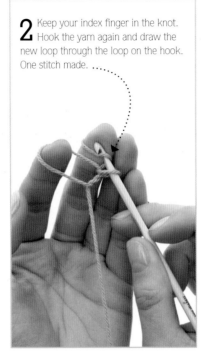

3 Put the hook back into the knot loop on your finger and pull another loop through. Draw another loop through this one. There are now two stitches on the hook.

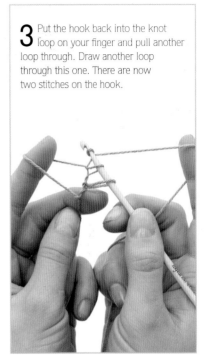

4 Repeat step 3, adding a loop to the hook each time until you have enough loops for a quarter of the required stitches. Remove your finger after the first few stitches. Transfer these stitches to the first knitting needle, and repeat to cast on a circle to four needles.

First four stitches on first needle

Yarn tail

5 When the project is complete, pull the yarn tail at the center and the hole will close neatly.

Pull yarn tail to close hole

Simple casting off

When your piece of knitted fabric is complete you need to close off the loops so that they can't unravel. This is called casting off (or binding off) the stitches. Although casting off is shown worked across knit stitches, the principle is the same for purl stitches. If instructed to retain stitches for future use, slip your stitches onto a spare needle or a stitch holder.

CASTING OFF KNITWISE

1 Begin by knitting the first two stitches. Then insert the tip of the left needle from left to right through the first stitch and lift this stitch up and over the second stitch and off the right needle.

2 To cast off the next stitch, knit one more stitch and repeat step 1. Continue until only one stitch remains on the right needle. (If your pattern says "cast off in pattern," work the stitches in the specified pattern as you cast off.)

3 To stop the last stitch from unraveling, cut the yarn, leaving a yarn tail 8in (20cm) long, which is long enough to darn into the knitting later. (Alternatively, leave a much longer yarn end to use for a future seam.) Pass the yarn end through the remaining loop and pull tight to close the loop. This is called fastening off.

SLIPPING STITCHES OFF NEEDLE

Stitch holder

Using a stitch holder: If you are setting stitches aside to work on later, your instructions will tell you whether to cut the yarn or keep it attached to the ball. Carefully slip your stitches onto a stitch holder large enough to hold all the stitches. If you are only slipping a few stitches, use a safety pin.

Using a length of yarn: If you don't have a stitch holder or don't have one large enough, you can use a length of cotton yarn instead. Using a blunt-ended yarn needle, pass the yarn through the stitches as you slip them off the knitting needle. Knot the ends of the cotton yarn together.

Alternative casting off

Try using one of these casting-off techniques to complement your project. Consider using a contrasting color, either in the basic cast-off or combined with a decorative style. Casting-off techniques are included that give more stretch to ribs or loosen an edge; adaptation of the three needle cast-off may even be used to join pockets and hems.

PURL CAST-OFF

1 Purl two stitches, then take yarn to back. Insert the tip of the left needle into the first stitch and pass it over the second stitch and off the right needle.

2 Bring yarn to front, repeat steps 1 and 2 across row, but purl only one stitch in Step 1. Pull end stitch through itself as for casting off knitwise (opposite).

CASTING OFF IN RIB EFFECT

Use on a single rib fabric to maintain the rib corrugations. This method adds a little more stretch than casting off in either all knit or all purl.

1 Work one knit and one purl. Yarn to back. Insert left needle into first stitch. Pass over second and off right needle.

2 Knit the next stitch then pass the first stitch over the second and off the right needle as before.

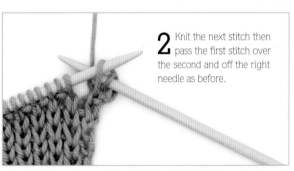

3 Yarn to front and purl next stitch. Repeat steps 2 and 3 across the row. Pull the final stitch through itself to fasten off.

SUSPENDED CAST-OFF (also called *delayed cast-off*)

This is ideal after lace knitting

1 Knit the first two stitches (this starts the row and is not repeated). Insert the left needle tip into the first stitch and pass it over the second and off the right tip. Do not drop it from the left tip.

2 Bring the right needle across the front of the "suspended" stitch, and knit the first stitch on the left needle.

3 Slip both loops off together as you complete the knit stitch. Continue passing and knitting stitches as in steps 1 and 2 to the end of the cast off.

CROCHET CAST-OFF

1 Hold the yarn in your left hand and keep it at the back. Slip the first stitch purlwise onto the crochet hook.

2 Insert the hook into the next stitch and drop it from the left needle. Catch yarn with hook and pull through both stitches. Repeat across the row, pulling the end loop through itself to fasten off.

THREE NEEDLE CAST-OFF

This seam can be worked on the right side of the knitting (as here) to form a decorative seam, or on the wrong side.

1 Hold the needles with the stitches to be joined together with the wrong sides facing each other. Insert a third needle through the center of the first stitch on each needle and knit these two stitches together.

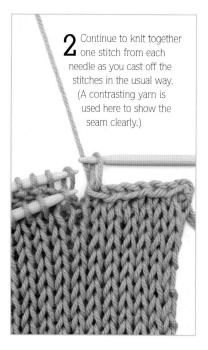

2 Continue to knit together one stitch from each needle as you cast off the stitches in the usual way. (A contrasting yarn is used here to show the seam clearly.)

3 When the pieces of knitting are opened out, you will see that this technique forms a raised chain along the seam.

PICOT POINT CAST-OFF

Where there is a seam, cast off the first stitch to leave a selvage before starting the picot edge.

1 Knit two stitches, insert the left needle into the first stitch on the right needle and pass it over the second stitch and off the right needle (casting off knitwise, see p. 50).

2 Slip the remaining right stitch onto the left needle without twisting it. Cast on two stitches by the cable cast-on method (see p. 37).

3 Cast off three stitches knitwise as described in step 1. Cast off another two stitches. (These form the straight edge between the picot points.)

4 Repeat steps 2–3 across the row.

5 A lamb's tail edge can be made by casting on more stitches in step 2 (the longer example shown has 20 stitches cast on). However many you choose, always cast off one more stitch in step 3 than you cast on. To make the tails twist, as shown center, cast off tighter than you cast on.

6 To use contrasting color for the picots, work the last row of the main fabric in contrast (purl row in stockinette stitch). To prevent the edge from rolling to the knit side, work the last two rows of the main fabric in garter stitch (see p. 59) or seed stitch (see p. 196). For a clean color join, introduce contrast yarn on the knit row before you start the garter or seed stitch. A picot cast-on can also be worked using this method of casting on and casting off the extra stitches between making each group of edge cast-on stitches (see pp. 36-37 for suitable cast-ons).

TWO ROW CAST-OFF

1 Work on an even number of stitches. Knit the first stitch and purl the second. With the yarn at the back, insert the left needle in the first stitch and pass it over the second stitch and off the right needle.

2 Knit and purl the next two stitches on the left needle. Take yarn to back. Pass the second (knit) stitch over the third (purl) stitch on the right needle to cast off one stitch.

3 Repeat step 2 across the row. This leaves you with half the number of original stitches on the needle. Cut the yarn leaving a tail. Do not turn the work.

4 Slip the last stitch on the right needle onto the left needle without twisting it; slip the next stitch in the same way. Pass the second stitch along on the left needle over the last stitch.

5 Repeat across the row, slipping only one stitch each time. Sew the last stitch in with a blunt-ended yarn needle and a separate piece of yarn.

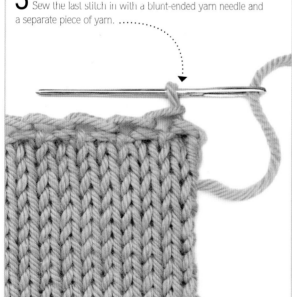

DECREASE CAST-OFF

A decorative cast-off, this is better for single ribs than plain casting off knitwise.

1 Insert the tip of the right needle into the front of the first two stitches on the left needle and knit them together. Slip the new stitch on the right needle back onto the left without twisting it. Repeat across the row, pulling the thread through the last stitch to secure the end.

VERY STRETCHY SINGLE RIB CAST-OFF

1 On a single rib fabric, make a yarn-over; then work the knit stitch at the start of the row.

2 Insert the left needle in the first stitch on the right needle. Lift it over the second stitch and off.

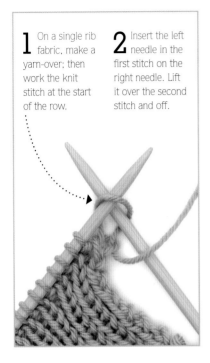

3 Bring yarn to front. Take yarn away from you over the top of the needle and back to the front. Purl the next stitch. There will be three stitches on the right needle.

4 Take yarn to back. Slip the first and second stitches on the right needle over the third and off.

5 Wrap the yarn around the needle and knit the next stitch. Slip the first and second stitches on the right needle over the third and off. Repeat steps 3–5 along the row.

EDGING CAST-OFF

For a contrast edge, work the last row of the main fabric in a contrasting color.

1 Cast on three stitches for edging on an empty right needle. Hold the needle with the stitches to cast off in your left hand. Slip the last stitch of the edging onto the left needle without twisting.

2 Knit the edging stitch and main color stitch by putting the right needle into the back of both stitches from above.

3 Turn the work, bring yarn to front. Slip the last stitch of the main fabric onto the left needle without twisting. Put the tip of the right needle into the back of both stitches from below, and purl together. Purl two remaining edging stitches.

4 Turn the work and knit all but one of the edging stitches, and then repeat steps 2 to 4.

CROCHET CHAIN LOOP CAST-OFF

This decorative cast-off helps prevent edges from stretching, particularly on lacy knitting.

1 The stitches should be divisible by four. Hold the stitches with the right side facing you in your left hand. Slip the first stitch onto a crochet hook.

2 Lay the yarn into the hook and pull it through to make a new chain; repeat until you have enough stitches to make a loop along the cast-off when it is stretched.

3 Insert the hook into the first four stitches on the needle. Slip them onto the hook. Lay yarn into the hook and pull a loop through all four stitches.

4 Lay yarn into the hook and make another chain through both loops on the hook. Repeat steps 2–4 across the edge, catching four stitches each time at step 3.

SMOOTH DIAGONAL CAST-OFF

This example assumes you are working a pattern with a diagonal edge to cast off in groups of five (such as a shoulder seam).

1 Cast off four stitches using the cast-off knitwise method (see p. 50), leaving the last stitch of the cast-off on the right needle.

2 Knit to the end of the row on the left needle, turn the work, and purl until there are only two stitches remaining on the left needle.

3 Purl these two stitches together. Turn the work. Repeat steps 2–4 until the cast off length is completed.

Working a knit stitch Abbreviation = *k*

All knitting is made up of two basic stitches—knit and purl. The knit stitch is shown here on stockinette stitch (see p. 59), which alternates rows of knit and purl stitches. Choose single, finger, or knit-on cast-on and start with garter stitch (see p. 59), which uses only knit stitch. Try out some fun stripes and experiment with different yarns before you learn purl stitch. The odd dropped stitch doesn't matter so much—put a safety pin through it so it doesn't drop further and sew it in later.

1 Hold the needle with the unworked stitches in your left hand and the other needle in your right hand, as explained on p. 33. With the yarn at the back of the knitting, insert the tip of the right needle from left to right under the front loop and through the center of the next stitch on the left needle.

Yarn at back of knitting

2 Wrap the yarn under and around the tip of the right needle, keeping an even tension as the yarn slips through your fingers.

3 With the tip of the right needle, carefully draw the yarn through the stitch on the left needle. Hold the yarn firmly but not too tightly.

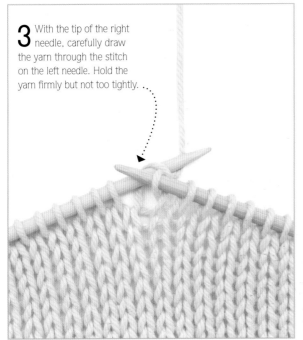

4 Let the old loop drop off the left needle to complete the knit stitch on the right needle. Work all the stitches on the left needle onto the right needle in the same way. To start a new row, turn the work and transfer the right needle to the left hand.

Old stitch

Completed new stitch

Working a purl stitch Abbreviation = p

The purl stitch (shown here on stockinette stitch [see p. 59]) is a little more difficult than knit stitch, but like knit stitch it becomes effortless after a little practice. Once you are a seasoned knitter, you will feel as if your hands would know how to work these basic stitches in your sleep. Work your first purl row after you have cast on and knitted a few rows of garter stitch. You may find your gauge alters when you purl, so try holding your yarn a little tighter or looser to compensate.

1 Hold the needle with the unworked stitches in your left hand and the other needle in your right hand as explained on p. 33. With the yarn at the front of the knitting, insert the tip of the right needle from right to left through the center of the next stitch to be worked on the left needle.

Yarn at front of knitting

2 Wrap the yarn over and around the tip of the right needle. Keep an even tension on the yarn as you release it through your fingers.

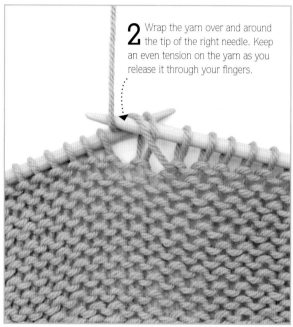

3 With the tip of the right needle, carefully draw the yarn through the stitch on the left needle. Keep your hands relaxed and allow the yarn to slip through your fingers in a gently controlled manner.

4 Let the old loop drop off the left needle to complete the purl stitch. Work all the stitches on the left needle onto the right needle in the same way. To start the next row, turn the work and transfer the knitting to the left hand.

Old stitch

Completed new stitch

Basic knit and purl stitches

Once you know how to work the knit and purl stitch with ease, you will be able to work the most frequently used stitch patterns—garter stitch, stockinette stitch, reverse stockinette stitch, and single ribbing. Stockinette stitch and reverse stockinette stitch are commonly used for plain knitted garments, and garter stitch and single ribbing for garment edgings.

GARTER STITCH (Abbreviation = *g st*)

Knit right-side (RS) rows: Garter stitch is the easiest of all knitted fabrics, since all rows are worked in knit stitches. When the right side of the fabric is facing you, knit all the stitches in the row.

Forms horizontal ridges

Edges of fabric lie flat and do not roll

Knit wrong-side (WS) rows: When the wrong side of the fabric is facing you, knit all the stitches in the row. The resulting fabric is soft, textured, and slightly stretchy.

Wrong side looks exactly like right side

STOCKINETTE STITCH (Abbreviation = *st st*)

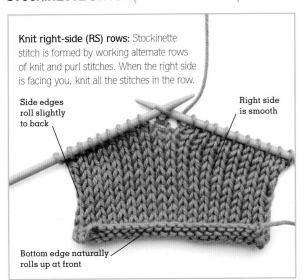

Knit right-side (RS) rows: Stockinette stitch is formed by working alternate rows of knit and purl stitches. When the right side is facing you, knit all the stitches in the row.

Side edges roll slightly to back

Right side is smooth

Bottom edge naturally rolls up at front

Purl wrong-side (WS) rows: When the wrong side is facing you, purl all the stitches in the row. The wrong side is often referred to as the "purl side" of the knitting.

Wrong side is knobbly

REVERSE STOCKINETTE STITCH (Abbreviation = *rev st st*)

Purl right-side (RS) rows:
Reverse stockinette stitch is
formed exactly like stockinette
stitch but the sides are reversed.
When the right side is facing you,
purl all the stitches in the row.

Right side
of fabric
is knobbly

Side edges roll
slightly to front

Bottom edge rolls
naturally up to back

Knit wrong side (WS) rows: When the wrong side
is facing you, knit all the stitches in the row.

Wrong side
of fabric
is smooth

SINGLE RIBBING (Abbreviation = *K1, P1 rib*)

Right-side (RS) rows: Single ribbing is formed
by working alternate knit and purl stitches. After
a knit stitch, take the yarn to the front of the
knitting between the two needles to purl the
next stitch. After a purl stitch, take the yarn
to the back between
the two needles to
knit the next stitch.

Ribbing has
vertical ridges
and is stretchy

Edges lie flat
and do not roll

Wrong-side (WS) rows: On the
wrong-side rows, knit all the knit
stitches that are facing you and
purl all the purl stitches. Work
the following rows in the same
way to form thin columns
of alternating single knit
and purl stitches.

Wrong side
looks exactly
like right side

Preparing and repairing

These useful tips will help both absolute beginners and more advanced knitters to prepare and complete their work with ease. Even experienced knitters can have problems joining on a new ball of yarn, and sewing in yarn ends correctly is the final touch for a professional finish.

Winding and joining yarns

Knowing how to wind a hank into a ball is a useful skill, especially since many luxury yarns are sold as hanks. Joining a new ball of yarn when the first has run out, or a color change is necessary, is a little daunting at first but easy to master.

WINDING A HANK INTO A BALL

1 Untwist the hank and carefully undo the knot joining the two ends of the yarn. Ask someone to hold the hank, or place it over a chair back. Pull out one of the yarn ends and wind it into a little yarn "butterfly" (see p. 63). Then pinch the butterfly together at the center and slip it off the left hand.

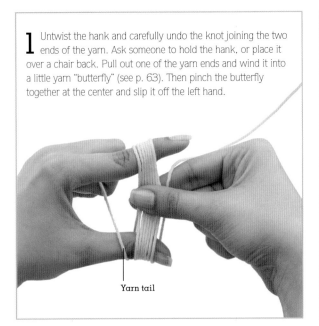

Yarn tail

2 Start wrapping the yarn around the butterfly and the thumb to create a hole in the center of the ball. Keep winding until the whole hank is used up. Be sure to change the positioning of the wraps frequently to keep the ball round. Secure the yarn end under a few of the outer wraps. When you start knitting, pull the butterfly out of the center and use this end. Pulling the yarn from inside stops the ball from rolling around.

To start using finished ball, pull butterfly from center

SQUARE KNOT

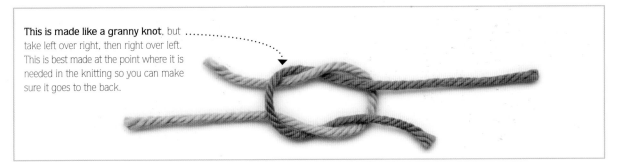

This is made like a granny knot, but take left over right, then right over left. This is best made at the point where it is needed in the knitting so you can make sure it goes to the back.

WEAVER'S KNOT

Use when joining yarns of different thicknesses.

1 Make a loop of the thick yarn and pinch the neck together. Thread a longish end of the thin yarn through the loop from above, and wrap it over the neck of the loop from back to front; pinch this to the loop with your fingers.

2 Take the thin yarn end that is wrapped around the loop under the front thread of the thick yarn loop. Pass it over itself as you take it toward the back and then pass it under the rear thread of the thick yarn loop.

3 Holding both thick yarns in one hand and both thin in the other, gently pull the short ends apart with your fingers to close the knot.

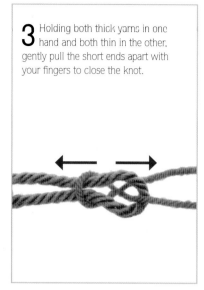

Joining on a new yarn

To calculate if there is enough yarn to complete two rows, fold the remaining yarn in half and make a slip knot at the fold. Knit the first row. If the knot comes before the end of the row you don't have enough yarn and need to join on a fresh ball.

JOINING ON A NEW BALL

1 Always join on a new ball at the beginning of a row. Knot the new end of yarn onto the old yarn.

End of old ball

New ball

2 Slide the knot up very close to the knitting. The knot can be hidden in the seam later. If you are knitting a scarf or blanket, tie the knot loosely so you can undo it later and darn in the ends.

Knot close to knitting

New ball joined on

JOINING ON A NEW YARN—ALTERNATIVE METHOD

1 Lay the new yarn over the right needle with the old yarn tail. Knit the first stitch of the new row with both yarns. Drop the old yarn tail and continue with the new.

Double stitch with both yarns

2 When the knitting is complete, rip out the second thread from the old yarn before darning the ends in with a blunt-ended yarn needle.

WINDING UP A LONG YARN TAIL

A long loose end on your slip knot can start to get tangled when it is packed away. To keep it neat, wind it into a yarn "butterfly" close to your knitting.

1 Starting close to the knitting, wrap the yarn around your thumb and forefinger in a figure-eight.

2 Remove the yarn "butterfly" from the thumb and forefinger and wrap the yarn end a few times around its center. Tuck the end under the wrapping to secure it.

Yarn end tucked under wrapping to secure

DARNING IN AN END

Freshly completed knitting will have at least two yarn ends dangling from it—one at the cast-on and one at the cast-off edges. For every extra ball used, there will be two more ends. Thread each end onto a blunt-ended needle and weave it vertically or horizontally through stitches on the wrong side of work.

Correcting mistakes

The best thing to do if you make a mistake in your knitting is to unravel it back to the mistake by ripping out the stitches one by one. If you drop a stitch, be sure to pick it up quickly before it comes undone right back to the cast-on edge.

RIPPING OUT A KNIT ROW

Hold the needle with the stitches in your right hand. To rip out each stitch individually, insert the tip of the left needle from front to back through the stitch below the first knit stitch on the right needle, then drop the old knit stitch off the needle and pull out the loop.

RIPPING OUT A PURL ROW

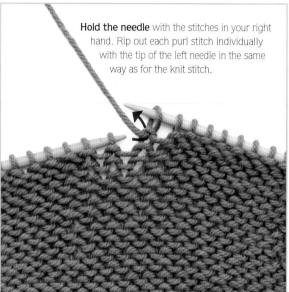

Hold the needle with the stitches in your right hand. Rip out each purl stitch individually with the tip of the left needle in the same way as for the knit stitch.

PICKING UP A DROPPED STITCH

If you drop a stitch on stockinette stitch, you can easily reclaim it with a crochet hook. With the right side of the knitting facing you, insert the hook through the dropped loop. Grab the strand between the stitches and pull a loop through the loop on the hook. Continue up the rows in this way until you reach the top. Then slip the stitch back onto your needle.

Following stitch patterns

Stitch pattern instructions are written or charted directions for making all kinds of textures—knit and purl combinations and cables. Knitting stitch pattern swatches is the best possible introduction to row instructions. Beginners should try some out before attempting to follow a complete knitting pattern (see pp. 68–69).

UNDERSTANDING WRITTEN INSTRUCTIONS

Anyone who can cast on, knit and purl, and cast off will be able to work from simple knit-and-purl-combination stitch pattern instructions with little difficulty. It is just a question of following the instructions one step at a time and getting used to the abbreviations. A list of common knitting abbreviations is given on p. 67, but for simple knit and purl textures all you need to grasp is that "k1" means "knit one stitch," "k2" means "knit two stitches," and so on. And the same applies for the purl stitches—"p1" means "purl one stitch," "p2" means "purl two stitches," and so on.

To begin a stitch pattern, cast on the number of stitches that it tells you to, using your chosen yarn and the yarn manufacturer's recommended needle size. Work the stitch row by row, then repeat the rows as instructed and the stitch pattern will grow beneath the needles. When your knitting is the desired size, cast off in pattern (see p. 50).

The best tips for first-timers are to follow the rows slowly; mark the right side of the fabric by knotting a colored thread onto it; use a row counter to keep track of where you are (see p. 23); and pull out your stitches and start again if you get mixed up. If you love the stitch pattern you are trying out, you can make a scarf, blanket, or pillow cover with it—no need to buy a knitting pattern.

The principles for following stitch patterns are the same for cables (see pp. 87–88), which you will be able to work once you learn cable techniques and how to increase and decrease.

Some stitch patterns will call for "slipping" stitches and knitting "through the back of the loop." These useful techniques are given next as a handy reference when you are consulting the abbreviations and terminology list.

SLIPPING STITCHES PURLWISE

1 Always slip stitches purlwise, for example, when slipping stitches onto a stitch holder, unless instructed otherwise. Insert the tip of the right needle from right to left through the front of the loop on the left needle.

2 Slide the stitch onto the right needle and off the left needle without working it. The slipped stitch now sits on the right needle with the right side of the loop at the front just like the worked stitches next to it.

SLIPPING STITCHES KNITWISE

1 Slip stitches knitwise if instructed to do so or if working decreases (see pp. 77–79), as it twists the stitch. First, insert the tip of the right needle from left to right through the front of the loop on the left needle.

2 Slide the stitch onto the right needle and off the left needle without working it. The slipped stitch now sits on the right needle with the left side of the loop at the front of the needle, unlike the worked stitches next to it.

KNITTING THROUGH BACK OF LOOP (Abbreviation = *k1 tbl*)

1 When row instructions say "k1 tbl" (knit one through the back of the loop), insert the right needle from right to left through the side of the stitch behind the left needle (called the back of the loop).

2 Wrap the yarn around the tip of the right needle and complete the knit stitch in the usual way. This twists the stitch in the row below so that the legs of the stitch cross at the base. (The same principle applies for working p1 tbl, k2tog tbl, and p2tog tbl.)

Crossed stitch

UNDERSTANDING STITCH SYMBOL CHARTS

Knitting instructions for stitch patterns can also be given in chart form. Some knitters prefer working from stitch symbol charts because they are easy to read, and they build up a visual image of the stitch repeat that is quick to memorize.

Even with charted instructions, there are usually written directions for how many stitches to cast on. If not, you can calculate the cast-on from the chart, where the number of stitches in the pattern "repeat" are clearly marked. Cast on a multiple of this number, plus any edge stitches outside the repeat.

Each square represents a stitch and each horizontal line of squares represents a row. After casting on, work from the bottom of the chart upward. Read odd-numbered rows (usually RS rows) from right to left and even-numbered rows (usually WS rows) from left to right. Work the edge stitches, then work the stitches inside the repeat as many times as required. Some symbols may mean one thing on a RS row and another on a WS row (see opposite).

Once you have worked all the charted rows, start again at the bottom of the chart to begin the "row repeat" once more.

3. Read row 2 and all other wrong-side rows from left to right

4. After completing row 16, start again at row 1

Rep = 16 rows

2. Read row 1 and all other right-side rows from right to left

Rep = 6 sts

3 edge sts

1. Cast on a multiple of 6 stitches, plus 3 extra stitches at each end

KNITTING ABBREVIATIONS

These are the most frequently used knitting abbreviations. Any special abbreviations in knitting instructions are always explained within the pattern.

alt	alternate	p2tog (or dec 1)	purl next 2sts together (see p. 77)	st(s)	stitch(es)
beg	begin(ning)	patt	pattern, or work in pattern	st st	stockinette stitch
cm	centimeter(s)			tbl	through the back loop(s)
cont	continu(e)(ing)	Pfb (or inc 1)	purl into front and back of next st (see p. 70)	tog	together
dec	decreas(e)(ing)			WS	wrong side (of work)
foll	follow(s)(ing)				
g	gram(s)	psso	pass slipped stitch over	wyib	with yarn in back
g st	garter stitch	rem	remain(s)(ing)	wyif	with yarn in front
in	inch(es)	rep	repeat(ing)	yd	yard(s)
inc	increas(e)(ing)	rev st st	reverse stockinette stitch	yo	yarn forward (UK yfwd; see p. 75)
k	knit	RS	right side (of work)		
k1 tbl	knit st through back of loop	s1 k1 psso (skp)	slip one, knit one, pass slipped st over (see p. 78)	yo	yarn forward around needle (UK yfrn; see p. 75)
k2tog (or dec 1)	knit next 2 sts together (see p. 77)	s1 k2tog psso (or sk2p)	slip one st, knit 2sts together, pass slipped sts over (see p. 79)	yo	yarn over needle (UK yon; see p. 75)
kfb (or inc 1)	knit into front and back of next st (see p. 70)	ssk	slip, slip, knit (see p. 78)	yo	yarn around needle (UK yrn; see p. 74)
m	meter(s)	sl	slip stitch(es)	[ ] *	Repeat instructions between brackets, or after or between asterisks, as many times as instructed
M1 (or M1k)	make one stitch (see pp. 71–73)	s2 k1 p2sso	slip 2, knit one, pass slipped stitches over (see p. 79)		
mm	millimeter(s)				
oz	ounce(s)				
p	purl				

KNITTING TERMINOLOGY AND SYMBOLS

The following terms are commonly used in knitting patterns. Where terminology differs between the US and UK, the UK equivalent is given in parentheses.

cast on Create a series of loops on a knitting needle to form the foundation for the piece of knitting.

cast off Close off stitches and drop from knitting needle (also: bind off).

cast off knitwise/purlwise Cast off while working stitches in knit/purl.

cast off in pattern Cast off while working stitches in the pattern used in the previous row.

cast off in ribbing Cast off while working stitches in the ribbing used in the previous row.

decrease Subtract the number of stitches in a row (see pp. 77–79).

garter stitch Knit one round and purl one round while knitting flat or knit every row in circular knitting (see p. 123).

gauge The size of the stitches in a piece of knitting (UK: tension), measured by the number of stitches and rows to 4in (10cm),

or to 1in (2.5cm) on fine knitting (see p. 69).

increase Add to the number of stitches in a row (see pp. 70–76).

knitwise Insert the right needle into the stitch on the left needle as if starting a knit stitch.

pick up and knit Draw loops through the edge of the knitting and place them on the needle (see p. 132).

purlwise Insert the right needle into the stitch on the left needle as if starting a purl stitch.

stockinette stitch Knit all RS rows and purl all WS rows (UK: stocking stitch).

reverse stockinette stitch Purl all RS rows and knit all WS rows (UK: reverse stocking stitch).

work even Work in specified pattern without increasing or decreasing (UK: work straight).

yarn-over increase Wrap yarn around right needle to make a new stitch; abbreviated yo (UK: yfwd, yfrn, yon, or yrn; see pp. 74–76).

STITCH SYMBOLS

These are some of the commonly used knitting symbols in this book. Any unusual symbols will be explained in the pattern. Symbols can vary, so follow the explanations in your pattern.

☐ = k on RS rows, p on WS rows

● = p on RS rows, k on WS rows

O = yarn over (see p. 74)

⟋ = k2tog (see p. 77)

⟍ = ssk (see p. 78)

⋀ = sk2p (see p. 79)

⟁ = s2k1 p2sso (see p. 79)

Following a pattern

Knitting patterns can look daunting to a beginner knitter, but, if approached step-by-step, they are easy to understand. This section provides an explanation of how to follow simple knitting patterns and gives tips for finishing details and seams.

Simple accessory patterns

The best advice for a beginner wanting to knit a first project from a knitting pattern is to start with a simple accessory. Pillow covers are especially good practice, since the instructions are straightforward and usually the only finishing details are seams. This is an example of a pattern for a simple striped stockinette-stitch pillow cover.

At the beginning of most patterns you will find the skill level required for the knitting. Make sure you are confident that the skill level is right for you.

Check the size of the finished item. If it is a simple square like this pillow, you can easily adjust the size by adding or subtracting stitches and rows.

Try to use the yarn specified. But if you are unable to obtain this yarn, choose a substitute yarn, as explained on p. 18.

Make a gauge swatch before starting to knit and change the needle size, if necessary (see opposite page).

Consult the abbreviations list with your pattern (or in your book) for the meanings of abbreviations (see p. 67).

If no stitch is specified for the cast-off, always cast off knitwise.

The back of a pillow cover is sometimes exactly the same as the front or it has a fabric back. In this case, the stripes are reversed on the back for a more versatile cover.

After all the knitted pieces are complete, follow the Finishing section of the pattern.

See p. 63 for how to darn in loose ends.

STRIPED PILLOW COVER

Skill level
Easy

Size of finished pillow
16 x 16in (40.5 x 40.5cm)

Materials
3 x 50g/137yd/125m balls in each of branded Pure Wool DK in Lavender 039 **(A)** and Avocado 019
(B) Pair of US size 6 (UK8/4mm) knitting needles
Pillow cushion to fit finished cover

Gauge
22 sts and 30 rows to 4in (10cm) over stockinette stitch using US size 6 (UK8/4mm) needles or size necessary to achieve correct gauge. To achieve correct measurements, take time to check gauge.

Front
Using US size 6 (UK8/4mm) needles and A, cast on 88 sts.
Beg with a K row, work in st st until work measures 5½in (14cm) from cast-on edge, ending with RS facing for next row.
Cut off A and change to B.
Cont in st st until work measures 10½in (26.5cm) from cast-on edge, ending with RS facing for next row.
Cut off B and change to A.
Cont in st st until work measures 16in (40.5cm) from cast-on edge, ending with RS facing for next row.
Cast off.

Back
Work as for Front, but use B for A, and A for B.

Finishing
Darn in loose ends.
Block and press lightly on wrong side, following instructions on yarn label.
With wrong sides facing, sew three sides of back and front together. Turn right-side out, insert Pillow cushion, and sew remaining seam.

Always purchase the same total amount in yards/meters of a substitute yarn; NOT the same amount in weight.

If desired, select different colors to suit your décor; the colors specified are just suggestions.

Alter the needle size if you cannot achieve the correct gauge with the specified size (see left).

Extra items needed for your project will usually be listed under Materials or Extras.

Instructions for working a piece of knitted fabric always start with how many stitches to cast on and what yarn or needle size to use. If there is only one needle size and one yarn, these may be absent here.

Work in the specified stitch pattern, for the specified number of rows or in/cm.

Colors are usually changed on a right-side row, so end with the right-side facing for the changeover row.

Make sure you look at the yarn label instructions before attempting to press any piece of knitting. The label may say that the yarn cannot be pressed or to press it only with a cool iron. (See p. 149 for blocking tips.)

See pp. 149–151 for seaming options. Take time with seams on knitting. Practice on odd pieces of knitting before starting the main project.

Garment patterns

Choosing the right size and knitting a gauge swatch are the two most important things to get right if you want to create a successful garment. It is also possible to make simple alterations to patterns worked in plain garter or stockinette stitch.

CHOOSING A GARMENT SIZE

Rather than looking at specific "sizes" when choosing which size to knit, select the one nearest to how you want the garment to fit. The best way to do this is to find a similar garment that fits you. Lay it flat and measure its width—choose the width on the pattern that is the closest match.

Photocopy your pattern and highlight the figures for your size throughout. Start with the number of balls of yarn, then the number of stitches to cast on, the length to knit to the armhole, and so on. The smallest size is given first and larger sizes follow in parentheses. Where only one figure is given, this applies to all sizes.

Choose your size by the width of a favorite, well-fitting sweater with the same shape and knitted fabric weight

Check that circumference of sleeve suits your upper arm measurement

Alter sweater length only where instructed

Alter sleeve length only where specified in instructions

ALTERING PATTERNS

You can alter the length of garment patterns worked in plain garter or stockinette stitch, but avoid altering armholes, necklines, or sleeve heads. Since sleeves and some bodies have shaping, this must also be adjusted. Make notes at every step. In this example, length is being added to a sleeve:

1 Copy, photocopy, or draw out the pattern diagram. Write the new required length on the diagram (e.g., 20in).

2 Find the number of rows to 4in in the gauge note. Divide that number by 4 to calculate how many rows there are in 1in. For example, 32 rows per 4in. 32 ÷ 4 = 8 rows per 1in.

3 Multiply the required new length by the number of rows in 1in. The resulting figure is the total number in the new length. For example, 20 × 8 = 160 rows.

4 Any increasing will also have to be recalculated. From the pattern,

note the number of stitches to cast on at the cuff and how many there will be on the needle just before the start of the underarm shaping (this figure should be shown at the end of the written instruction for the increases).

5 Subtract the smallest from the largest amount of stitches. The answer is the total number of stitches to be increased. Divide the answer by two (because a sleeve has two sides), to give the number of stitches to increase on each side. For example, 114 - 60 = 54 sts. 54 ÷ 2 = 27 sts.

6 To calculate the number of rows between each increase, divide the new number of rows found in Step 3 by the number of increases calculated in Step 5. If you have a fraction in this answer, round the number down. For example, 144 ÷ 27 = 4.22. Increase one stitch each side every 4 rows. Knit the remainder rows straight before underarm cast-offs.

Measuring gauge

Always knit a swatch before starting your knitting in order to make sure that you can achieve the stitch size (gauge) recommended in your pattern. Only if you achieve the correct gauge will your finished knitted pieces have the correct measurements.

1 Using the specified needle size, knit a swatch about 5in (13cm) square. Mark 4in (10cm) across the center of your swatch with pins and count the number of stitches between the pins.

2 Count the number of rows to 4in (10cm) in the same way. If you have fewer stitches and rows than you should, try again with a smaller needle size; if you have more, change to a larger needle size. Use the needle size for your knitting that best matches the correct gauge. (Matching stitch width is more important than matching row height.)

Increases and decreases

Increasing and decreasing the number of stitches on the needle is the way knitting is shaped, changing the edges from straight vertical sides to curves and slants. But increases and decreases are also used in combinations with plain knit and purl stitches to form interesting textures in the knitted fabric.

Simple increases

The following techniques are simple increases used for shaping knitting. They create one extra stitch without creating a visible hole and are called invisible increases. Multiple increases, which add more than one extra stitch, are used less frequently and are always explained fully in the knitting pattern—one is given here as an example.

KNIT INTO FRONT AND BACK OF STITCH (Abbreviation = *kfb* or *inc 1*)

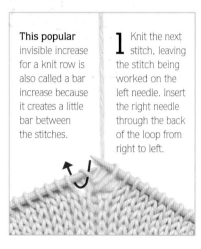

This popular invisible increase for a knit row is also called a bar increase because it creates a little bar between the stitches.

1 Knit the next stitch, leaving the stitch being worked on the left needle. Insert the right needle through the back of the loop from right to left.

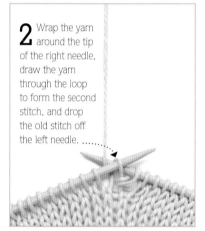

2 Wrap the yarn around the tip of the right needle, draw the yarn through the loop to form the second stitch, and drop the old stitch off the left needle.

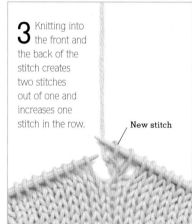

3 Knitting into the front and the back of the stitch creates two stitches out of one and increases one stitch in the row.

New stitch

PURL INTO FRONT AND BACK OF STITCH (Abbreviation = *pfb* or *inc 1*)

1 Purl the next stitch, leaving the stitch being worked on the left needle. Insert the right needle through the back of the loop from left to right.

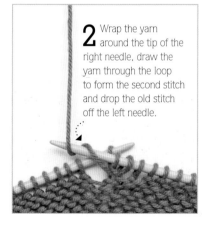

2 Wrap the yarn around the tip of the right needle, draw the yarn through the loop to form the second stitch and drop the old stitch off the left needle.

3 Purling into the front and the back of the stitch like this creates two stitches out of one and increases one stitch in the row.

New stitch

LIFTED INCREASE ON KNIT ROW (Abbreviation = *inc 1*)

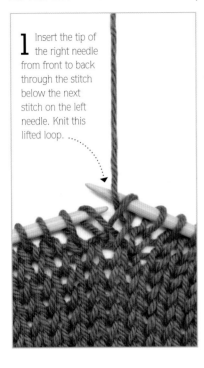

1 Insert the tip of the right needle from front to back through the stitch below the next stitch on the left needle. Knit this lifted loop. ....

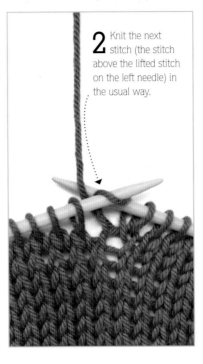

2 Knit the next stitch (the stitch above the lifted stitch on the left needle) in the usual way.

3 This creates two stitches out of one and increases one stitch in the row. (The purl version of this stitch is worked using the same principle.)

New stitch

"MAKE-ONE" LEFT LEANING INCREASE ON A KNIT ROW (Abbreviation = *M1* or *M1k*)

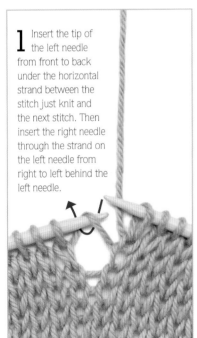

1 Insert the tip of the left needle from front to back under the horizontal strand between the stitch just knit and the next stitch. Then insert the right needle through the strand on the left needle from right to left behind the left needle.

2 Wrap the yarn around the tip of the right needle and draw the yarn through the lifted loop. (This is called knitting through the back of the loop.)

3 This creates an extra stitch in the row. (Knitting through the back of the loop twists the base of the new stitch to produce a crossed stitch that closes up the hole it would have created.)

New stitch slants to the left

Increases and decreases **71**

"MAKE-ONE" RIGHT LEANING INCREASE ON A KNIT ROW (Abbreviation = M1 or M1k)

Patterns do not always differentiate between left and right "make-one" increases. Choose the most suitable for your project.

1 Insert the tip of the left needle from back to front under the horizontal strand between the stitch just knit and the next stitch. Insert the right needle from left to right into the front of this new loop, twisting the stitch.

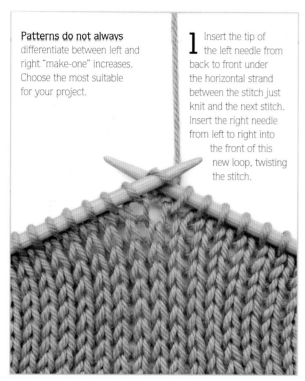

2 Wrap the yarn around the tip of the needle and draw the yarn through the lifted loop, knitting into the front of the stitch.

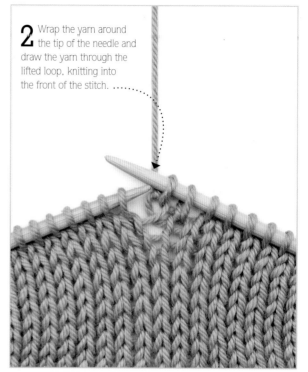

3 This action crosses the lifted stitch and closes the hole made by picking up the loop. The resulting increase slants to the right and is normally worked at the end of a knit row.

Slants to the right

"MAKE-ONE" INCREASE ON PURL ROW (Abbreviation = *M1* or *M1p*)

1 Insert the tip of the left needle from front to back under the horizontal strand between the stitch just knit and the next stitch. Then insert the right needle through the strand on the left needle from left to right behind the left needle.

2 Wrap the yarn around the tip of the right needle and draw the yarn through the lifted loop (known as purling through the back of the loop.)

3 This creates an extra stitch in the row. (Purling through the back of the loop twists the base of the new stitch to produce a crossed stitch that closes up the hole it would have created.)

— New stitch

MULTIPLE INCREASES (Abbreviation = *[k1, p1, k1] into next st*)

This is a very easy increase if you need to add more than one stitch to an existing stitch, but it does create a small hole under the new stitches.

1 To begin the increase, knit the next stitch but leave the old stitch on the left needle. ....

2 Then purl and knit into the same loop on the left needle. This action is called knit one, purl one, knit one all into the next stitch. It creates two extra stitches in the row. You can keep alternating k and p stitches in the same loop to create more stitches if desired.

k1
p1
k1

Yarn-over increases

Yarnover increases add stitches to a row and create holes at the same time, so are often called visible increases. They are used to produce decorative laces. A yarn-over is made by looping the yarn around the right needle to form an extra stitch. It is important to wrap the loop around the needle in the correct way or it will become crossed when it is worked in the next row, which closes the hole.

YARN-OVER BETWEEN KNIT STITCHES (Abbreviation = *yo*)

1 Bring the yarn to the front of the knitting between the needles. Take the yarn over the top of the right needle to the back and work the next knit stitch in the usual way.

2 When the knit stitch is complete, the yarn-over is correctly formed on the right needle with the right leg of the loop at the front.

Completed yarn-over increase

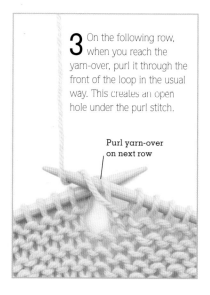

3 On the following row, when you reach the yarn-over, purl it through the front of the loop in the usual way. This creates an open hole under the purl stitch.

Purl yarn-over on next row

YARN-OVER BETWEEN PURL STITCHES (Abbreviation = *yo*)

1 Bring the yarn to the back of the work over the top of the right needle, then to the front between the needles. Work the next purl stitch in the usual way.

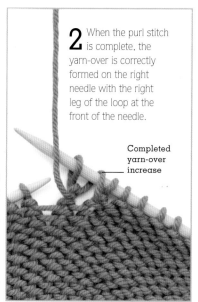

2 When the purl stitch is complete, the yarn-over is correctly formed on the right needle with the right leg of the loop at the front of the needle.

Completed yarn-over increase

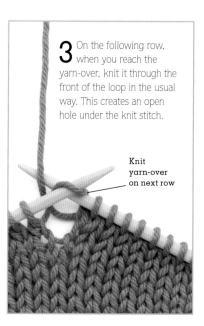

3 On the following row, when you reach the yarn-over, knit it through the front of the loop in the usual way. This creates an open hole under the knit stitch.

Knit yarn-over on next row

YARN-OVER BETWEEN KNIT AND PURL STITCHES (Abbreviation = *yo*)

After a knit stitch and before a purl stitch: Bring the yarn to the front between the needles, then over the top of the right needle and to the front again. Purl the next stitch. On the following row, work the yarn-over through the front of the loop in the usual way to create an open hole.

Yarn-over increase

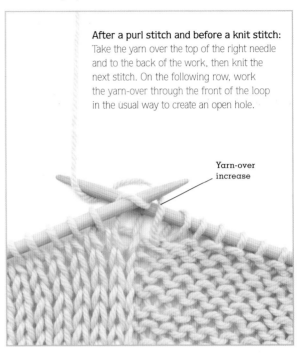

After a purl stitch and before a knit stitch: Take the yarn over the top of the right needle and to the back of the work, then knit the next stitch. On the following row, work the yarn-over through the front of the loop in the usual way to create an open hole.

Yarn-over increase

YARN-OVER AT THE BEGINNING OF A ROW (Abbreviation = *yo*)

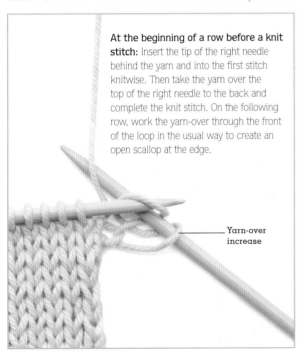

At the beginning of a row before a knit stitch: Insert the tip of the right needle behind the yarn and into the first stitch knitwise. Then take the yarn over the top of the right needle to the back and complete the knit stitch. On the following row, work the yarn-over through the front of the loop in the usual way to create an open scallop at the edge.

Yarn-over increase

At the beginning of a row before a purl stitch: Wrap the yarn from front to back over the top of the right needle and to the front again between the needles. Then purl the first stitch. On the following row, work the yarn-over through the front of the loop in the usual way to create an open scallop at the edge.

Yarn-over increase

DOUBLE YARN-OVER (Abbreviation = *yo2* or *yo* twice)

1 For a double yarn-over between two knit stitches, take the yarn over the top of the right needle to the back of the work, between the needles to the front again, and over the top of the right needle to the back again, ready to knit the next stitch.

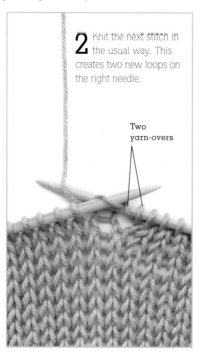

2 Knit the next stitch in the usual way. This creates two new loops on the right needle.

Two yarn-overs

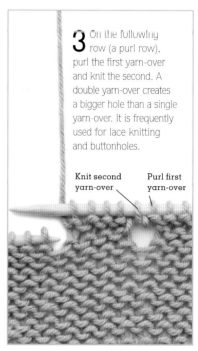

3 On the following row (a purl row), purl the first yarn-over and knit the second. A double yarn-over creates a bigger hole than a single yarn-over. It is frequently used for lace knitting and buttonholes.

Knit second yarn-over

Purl first yarn-over

CLOSED YARN-OVER ON GARTER STITCH

1 This is used as an "invisible" increase and is especially good for garter stitch. Take the yarn from back to front over the top of the right needle, then around the needle to the back of the work between the needles. Knit the next stitch in the usual way.

Yarn-over increase

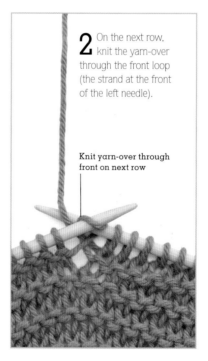

2 On the next row, knit the yarn-over through the front loop (the strand at the front of the left needle).

Knit yarn-over through front on next row

3 This creates a crossed stitch and closes the yarn-over hole. Although the crossed stitch is similar to the one made with a make-one increase (see p. 71), it is looser, which is perfect for the loose garter stitch texture.

Completed closed yarn-over

Simple decreases

These simple decreases are often used for shaping knitting and, paired with increases, for textured and lace stitches. More complicated decreases are always explained in knitting instructions. Most of the decreases that follow are single decreases that subtract only one stitch from the knitting, but a few double decreases are included.

KNIT TWO TOGETHER (Abbreviation = *k2tog* or *dec 1*)

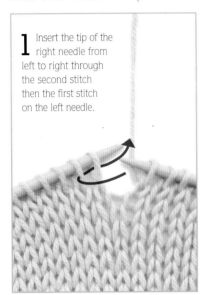

1 Insert the tip of the right needle from left to right through the second stitch then the first stitch on the left needle.

2 Wrap the yarn around the tip of the right needle, draw the yarn through both loops and drop the old stitches off the left needle.

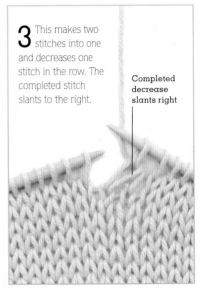

3 This makes two stitches into one and decreases one stitch in the row. The completed stitch slants to the right.

Completed decrease slants right

PURL TWO TOGETHER (Abbreviation = *p2tog* or *dec 1*)

1 Use the p2tog decrease where a pattern specifies "decrease 1" on a purl row. Insert the tip of the right needle from right to left through the first then the second stitch on the left needle.

2 Wrap the yarn around the tip of the right needle, draw the yarn through both loops and drop the old stitches off the left needle.

3 This makes two stitches into one and decreases one stitch in the row.

Completed decrease slants right on right side of work

SLIP ONE, KNIT ONE, PASS SLIPPED STITCH OVER (Abbreviation = *s1 k1 psso* or *skp*)

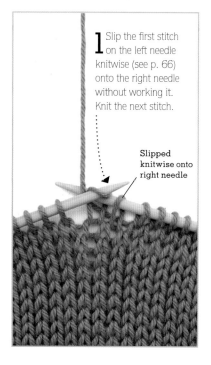

1 Slip the first stitch on the left needle knitwise (see p. 66) onto the right needle without working it. Knit the next stitch.

Slipped knitwise onto right needle

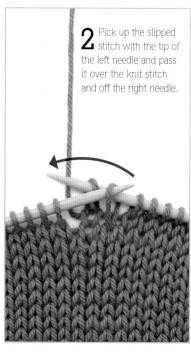

2 Pick up the slipped stitch with the tip of the left needle and pass it over the knit stitch and off the right needle.

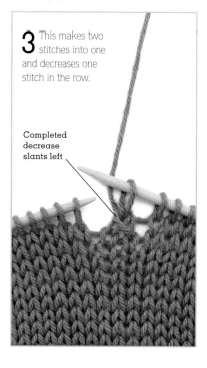

3 This makes two stitches into one and decreases one stitch in the row.

Completed decrease slants left

SLIP, SLIP, KNIT (Abbreviation = *ssk*)

1 Slip the next two stitches on the left needle knitwise (see p. 66), one at a time, onto the right needle without working them.

Slipped knitwise onto right needle

2 Insert the tip of the left needle from left to right through the fronts of the two slipped stitches (the right needle is now behind the left). Knit these two stitches together.

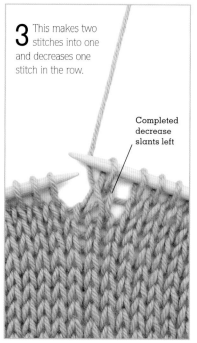

3 This makes two stitches into one and decreases one stitch in the row.

Completed decrease slants left

SLIP, SLIP, PURL (Abbreviation = *ssp*)

1 Keeping yarn at the front, slip two stitches, one at a time, knitwise (see p. 66) onto the right needle without working them as for ssk decrease.

2 Holding the needles tip to tip, insert the left needle into both stitches and transfer back to the left needle without twisting them.

3 Holding the right needle at the back, bring the tip upward from left to right through the back of the two stitches, bringing the right needle in front of the left as it comes through the stitches.

4 Lay the yarn between the needles as for purl. Take the right needle down and back through both loops, then slide them off the left needle together. This makes one stitch out of the two, and decreases one stitch.

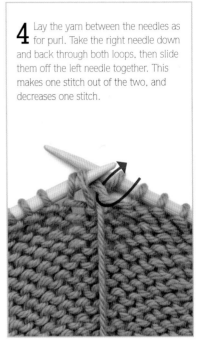

DOUBLE DECREASES

k3tog: Insert the tip of the right needle from left to right through the third stitch on the left needle, then the second, then the first. Knit these three together. This decreases two stitches at once.

Top stitch in decrease slants right

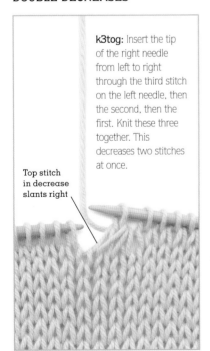

s1 k2tog psso (or sk2p): Slip one stitch knitwise onto the right needle, knit the next two stitches together, then pass the slipped stitch over the k2tog and off the right needle. This decreases two stitches at once.

Top stitch in decrease slants left

s2k k1 p2sso: Slip two stitches knitwise together onto the right needle, knit the next stitch, then pass the two slipped stitches together over the knit stitch and off the right needle. This decreases two stitches at once.

Top stitch in decrease is upright

Paired increases and decreases

Increases or decreases at each end of a row can be worked to slant left or right so that the edges mirror each other. Paired shapings should be worked at consistent intervals, and are easier if worked on a knit row. When working a pattern, one or two edge stitches can be worked plain so that the shaping does not affect the pattern.

SUMMARY OF INCREASES AND DECREASES

PAIRED INCREASES			
When made at end of a row	Abbreviation	When made at beginning of a row	Abbreviation
Slants left—increases the left edge of the knit side of stockinette stitch		Slants right—shapes the right edge of the knit side of stockinette stitch	
Left lifted increase	inc1	Right lifted increase	inc1
• virtually invisible • must have rows between or will pull • shows to right of increased stitch—slants the original stitch to the left and toward the selvage when used for edge shaping		• virtually invisible • must have rows between or will pull • shows to left of increased stitch—slants the original stitch to the right and toward the selvage when used for edge shaping	
Knit (or purl) in front and back of stitch	kfb or inc1	Knit (or purl) in front and back of stitch	kfb or inc1
Purl in front and back increases: • on a purl row seen from knit side, bar to the right of the stitch into which increase is made		Knit in front and back increases: • on a knit row seen from knit side, bar to the left of the stitch into which increase is made	
Left leaning increase	M1k (M1p)	Right leaning increase	M1k (M1p)
• virtually invisible • must have rows between or will pull • made between stitches, so shows where placed • slants the stitch worked after it to the left		• virtually invisible • must have rows between or will pull • made between stitches, so shows where placed • slants the stitch worked before it to the right	

PAIRED DECREASES			
When made at end of a row	Abbreviation	When made at start of a row	Abbreviation
Right slant—decreases the left of the knit side of stockinette stitch		Left slant—decreases the right of the knit side of stockinette stitch	
Knit (or purl) two together	k2tog (p2tog)	Slip, slip, knit (or slip, slip, purl)	ssk (ssp)
Knit (or purl) two together	k2tog (p2tog)	Slip1, knit1, pass slipped stitch over	skp, s1 K1 psso, or skpo
Knit (or purl) two together	k2tog (p2tog)	Knit (or purl) two together through back of loops	k2tog tbl (p2tog tbl) or k-b2tog (p-b2tog)

PAIRED LIFTED EDGE INCREASE

This example increases each side of stockinette stitch using a right lifted increase (see p. 71) at the start, and its paired left lifted increase at the end of every alternate knit row.

1 On an increase row, knit one stitch. Make a right lifted increase by inserting the tip of the right needle from front to back into the right side of the stitch below the next stitch on the left needle (be careful not to catch more than one strand of yarn). Knit this lifted loop.

2 Knit to the last but one stitch of the row. Make a left lifted increase by inserting the left needle tip from front to back into the left side of the stitch, two rows below the new stitch on the right needle. Knit this loop, and knit the last stitch.

Slants to left

3 If you find the left lifted increase awkward, pick the loop up with the left needle from back to front, slip it onto the right needle, twisting it as it is returned to the left. Knit into the front of the loop.

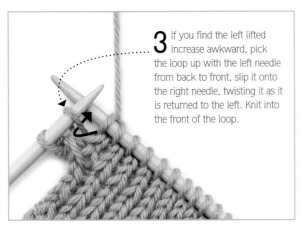

4 The paired increases look like this when completed over a number of rows.

PAIRED EDGE DECREASES (Abbreviation = *skp* and *k2tog*)

This example has decreases on each side of stockinette stitch. It has a slip1, knit1, pass slipped stitch over (skp) at the beginning of the row, which is paired with knit two together (k2tog) at the end of the row. Slip, slip, knit (ssk) may be substituted for skp, if preferred.

1 At the start of a knit row, work a slip1, knit1, psso as shown on p. 78.

2 Knit to two stitches from the end of the row and knit two stitches together as shown on p. 77.

"k2tog" slants to the right on left edge

"skp" slants to the left on right edge

Fully fashioned shaping

This is a method of increasing or decreasing the width of stockinette stitch while preserving a line of stitches that follow the outline of the piece. This looks attractive and makes sewing up easier. Use "paired" increases and decreases on a symmetrical piece: a left slope decrease must be mirrored by a right sloping one at the other side.

ON A KNIT ROW (Abbreviation = *ssk* and *k2tog*)

This example decreases one stitch at each end of a knit row but leaves two plain stitches at the selvage.

1 Knit the first two stitches. Slip the next two stitches knitwise, one by one onto the right needle. Insert the left needle from left to right through the front of both stitches and knit together. This is a left-slanting ssk decrease (see p. 78).

2 Knit to four stitches from the end of the row. Knit two stitches together (see p. 77) and then knit the last two stitches. This slopes to the right.

"k2tog" on stitches slanting to right on left edge

"ssk" on stitches slanting to left on right edge

ON A PURL ROW (Abbreviation = *ssp* and *p2tog*)

This example decreases one stitch at each end of a purl row but leaves two plain stitches at the selvage.

1 Purl the first two stitches. Slip the next two stitches one at a time knitwise onto the right needle. Slip them back together without twisting (purlwise). Insert the right needle into the front of both stitches from the right and purl them together (ssp). This slopes to the right.

2 Work to five stitches from the end, purl two stitches together (see p. 77) and purl the last three stitches. This slopes to the left. Ssk and ssp work better than other decreases when paired with k2tog or p2tog.

"ssp" on stitches slanting to right on left edge

"p2tog" on stitches slanting to left on right edge

Decorative central increases and decreases

Although paired increases and decreases are most commonly used for edge shaping in knitting, they become highly decorative as well as functional when worked closely together within the main fabric. For example, central decreases might be spaced around a flared peplum as part of the pattern, while central increases could emphasize waist-to-bust darting. Decorative central decreases are sometimes combined with yarn-over increases in more complex lace patterns.

KNIT INTO FRONT AND BACK AS A PAIRED CENTRAL INCREASE (Abbreviation = *kfb*)

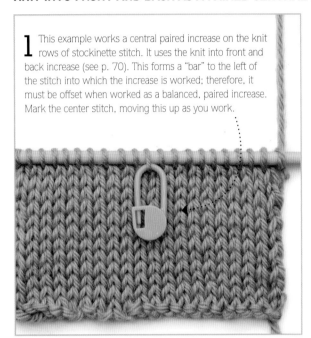

1 This example works a central paired increase on the knit rows of stockinette stitch. It uses the knit into front and back increase (see p. 70). This forms a "bar" to the left of the stitch into which the increase is worked; therefore, it must be offset when worked as a balanced, paired increase. Mark the center stitch, moving this up as you work.

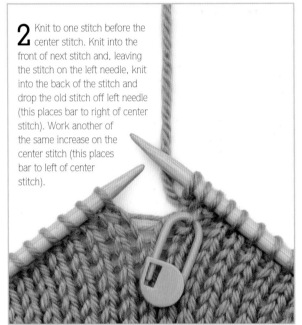

2 Knit to one stitch before the center stitch. Knit into the front of next stitch and, leaving the stitch on the left needle, knit into the back of the stitch and drop the old stitch off left needle (this places bar to right of center stitch). Work another of the same increase on the center stitch (this places bar to left of center stitch).

3 Knit to the end of the row. Purl one complete row, and repeat the increase sequence. This increase can be made in a similar manner into a purl stitch, in which case the bar lies to the right of the stitch.

4 This increase can be used in fully fashioned shaping (see opposite), in which case work the increase on the second stitch from the beginning of the row and the third from the end to leave two stitches symmetrically along the selvages.

OPEN CENTRAL INCREASE

1 On the purl row before the increase, make a yarn-over at the position of the increase. Knit to the increase position on the next row. Knit into the back of the yarn-over, and drop the yarn-over off the left needle.

2 Insert the left needle back into the dropped loop from back left so it is twisted as shown, and knit into the front of the loop.

3 Repeat steps 1 and 2 as you work up the piece. This increases two stitches every other row.

CLOSED CENTRAL INCREASE

1 Work the row, stopping before knitting the central stitch. Knit into the back and front of the central stitch and slide off the left needle. Gently pull the yarn to tighten the last stitch.

2 Look for the vertical strand stretching downward immediately to the right of this stitch. Insert the tip of the left needle from the left into this strand and knit into the back of the loop.

3 Knit to the end of the row. Purl the next row. Repeat steps 1–3, remembering that there will be one more stitch to knit on each row before working the increase.

RAISED CENTRAL DECREASE

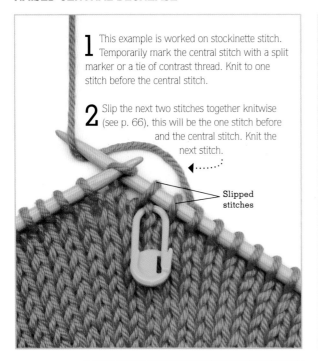

1 This example is worked on stockinette stitch. Temporarily mark the central stitch with a split marker or a tie of contrast thread. Knit to one stitch before the central stitch.

2 Slip the next two stitches together knitwise (see p. 66), this will be the one stitch before and the central stitch. Knit the next stitch.

Slipped stitches

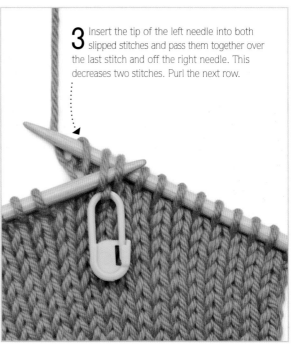

3 Insert the tip of the left needle into both slipped stitches and pass them together over the last stitch and off the right needle. This decreases two stitches. Purl the next row.

4 To ensure that the decrease remains central, on each knit row work to one stitch before the raised center stitch.

5 Repeat steps 2 and 3 as required.

FLAT CENTRAL DECREASE

1 This example is worked on stockinette stitch. Working only on knit rows, knit to one stitch from the central stitch. Temporarily mark the central stitch with a split marker or a tie of contrast thread. Slip the next stitch knitwise (see p. 66).

2 Insert the right needle knitwise through the next two stitches at once, and knit them together.

3 Insert the left needle into the second stitch on the right needle and pass it over the last stitch and off the needle. Knit to the end of the row.

4 To keep the decrease central, knit to one stitch before the central stitch of the decrease below before repeating steps 1–3. This technique decreases one stitch each side of the central stitch.

Cables and twists

Many interesting textures can be created by combining knit and purl stitches in various sequences (see pp. 196–198), but if you are looking for textures with higher relief and more sculptural qualities, cables and twists are the techniques to learn. Both are made by crossing stitches over each other in different ways to form an array of intricate patterns.

Simple twists

A simple twist is made over only two stitches, without a cable needle. Although twists do not create such high relief as cables, their ease and subtlety make them very popular. The following twists are worked in stockinette stitch on a stockinette stitch ground. They can also be worked with one knit and one purl stitch—the principle is the same.

RIGHT TWIST (Abbreviation = *T2R*)

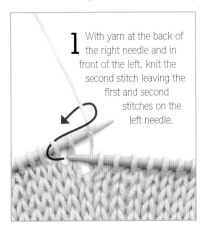

1 With yarn at the back of the right needle and in front of the left, knit the second stitch leaving the first and second stitches on the left needle.

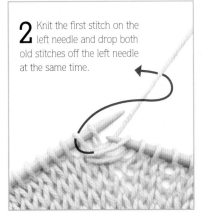

2 Knit the first stitch on the left needle and drop both old stitches off the left needle at the same time.

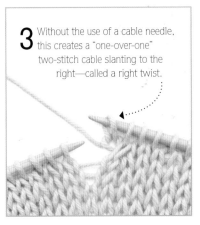

3 Without the use of a cable needle, this creates a "one-over-one" two-stitch cable slanting to the right—called a right twist.

LEFT TWIST (Abbreviation = *T2L*)

1 Insert the tip of the right needle behind the first stitch on the left needle and through the second stitch knitwise. Wrap the yarn around the right needle.

2 Pull the loop through the second stitch behind the first stitch. Be careful not to drop either the first or second stitches off the left needle yet.

3 Knit the first stitch on the left needle and drop both old stitches off the left needle. This creates a two-stitch cable slanting to the left—called a left twist.

Cables

Cables are usually worked in stockinette stitch on a reverse stockinette stitch (or garter stitch) ground. They are made by crossing two, three, four or more stitches over other stitches in the row. This technique is illustrated here with the cable 4 front and cable 4 back cables, which are crossed on every sixth row.

CABLE 4 FRONT (Abbreviation = *C4F*)

1 Work to the position of the four stockinette stitches that form the cable and slip the first two stitches onto a cable needle. With the cable needle at the front, knit the next two stitches on the left needle. ....▶

2 Next, knit the two stitches from the cable needle. ....▼

3 This creates a cable crossing that slants to the left. For this reason, a "front" cable is also called a "left" cable.

CABLE 4 BACK (Abbreviation = *C4B*)

1 Work as for step 1 of cable 4 front, but knit the first two stitches from the left needle with the cable needle at the back of the knitting.

2 Knit the two stitches from the cable needle. ....▼

3 This creates a cable crossing that slants to the right. For this reason, a "back" cable is also called a "right" cable.

I-cord

I-cord stands for "idiot" cord and is also known as slip cord. It is knitted on double-pointed needles and makes a neat edging or can be used for straps and ties, or for appliqué in a contrasting color. Use smaller needles for a tighter edge and work in a tight gauge.

Free form I-cord

These cords can be applied to an item later, so it is possible to add extra detail as they are worked. Stripes, texture, structural effects, and even beads can be incorporated. With its simple method but multiple uses, I-cord is a very versatile technique.

SIMPLE I-CORD—FOR APPLIQUÉ, TIES, AND STRAPS

1 Cast on five stitches using the backward loop cast-on shown on p. 35. Knit one row.

2 Transfer the needle to your left hand without turning it, and slide all the stitches to the right end of the needle, so that the yarn appears to be at the wrong end to knit another row.

3 Insert the right needle into the first stitch on the left needle, pull the yarn firmly from the left side of the knitting around the back to knit the first stitch. Tug the yarn again to pull the knitting around into a tube.

4 Repeat steps 2 and 3 until the cord is the required length.

SPIRAL I-CORD

This version works up shorter than simple I-cord, but is stretchier.

1 Cast on three stitches using the backward loop or cable cast-on method (see pp. 35 and 37). Knit one row. Continue as for simple I-cord (see above), but purl the next row. Repeat, alternating knit and purl rows to the required length.

TWO COLOR I-CORD

1 Cast on five stitches using backward loop cast-on (see p. 35). Knit the first stitch in the main color.

2 Insert the right needle into the second stitch and lay the contrast yarn between the needles. Knit the second stitch.

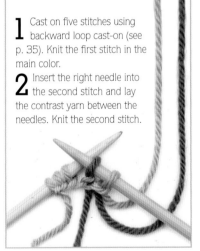

3 Drop the contrast, pick up the main color, and knit the third stitch. Repeat, alternating colors, ending with main color.

4 Slide stitches to other end of needle as in simple I-cord (above). Keeping the colors in sequence, knit next row. Repeat steps 2–4 to required length. See techniques for holding the yarns on pp. 98—99.

Attached I-cord

Attaching I-cords as you work saves time when sewing up later on. I-cords can be added to a finished piece for edging, or form part of the main project as a cast-off or edge. Their use as button loops and soft buttons add attractive and unique finishes to garments.

I-CORD EDGING

1 Cast on between two and five stitches. Knit one row. Transfer the needle to your left hand. Slide stitches as for simple I-cord (see p. 89).

2 Pull yarn around back of stitches and knit all but the last stitch of the next row. Slip the remaining stitch knitwise from left to right needle.

3 With empty left needle, pick up the extreme right loop of the lowest stitch on the main fabric edge from left to right. (This ensures the stitch is correctly positioned for the next step.)

4 Hold the needle with I-cord to the right of the edge of the main fabric. Knit the stitch on the left needle onto the right one. There will now be one extra stitch on the right needle. Insert the left needle into the second stitch on the right needle (slipped stitch) and pass it over the first stitch.

5 Repeat steps 2–4. Tip: To smoothly join i-cord end to end, graft across open stitches. When edging curves, use a larger needle in the right hand, reverting to original size on straight sections.

I-CORD BUTTON LOOP

1 Leave a tail of yarn four times the selvage length. Using a circular needle and the yarn tail, pick up the selvage (right side facing). Return to the starting end of the needle, and cast on three stitches using cable cast-on (p.37).

2 Knit two stitches. Work an ssk with last I-cord stitch and next picked up stitch.

3 Slip the three I-cord stitches to left needle without twisting (or use two double pointed needles). Work I-cord edging to the starting point of the button loop. Knit the three I-cord stitches, then slip them onto left needle. Continue with unattached I-cord until loop is correct size for button. Join I-cord to main fabric as in step 2.

I-CORD CAST-OFF

1 If the I-cord is to be in a contrasting color, work the last row of the main piece in the contrast yarn. Holding work to be cast off in the left hand, add three stitches to left needle using cable cast-on (see p. 37).

2 Knit two stitches. Slip the next two stitches (last of I-cord and first of edge stitches) onto the right needle one by one knitwise. Insert a double-pointed needle from left to right into the front of both stitches and knit together (ssk).

3 Slip the three stitches on the double-pointed needle to the opposite end. Repeat steps 2 and 3 to end of cast-off. This technique is worked the same on the purl side of the work. Work loosely, since I-cord can pucker the cast-off edge if worked too tightly.

I-CORD BOBBLE

1 At the bobble position, drop the straight right needle (use a point protector to hold stitches, if necessary). With a double-pointed needle, knit into the front, back, front, and back again of the next stitch.

2 Slide stitches to the opposite end of the needle. Pull yarn across back and knit the four stitches again; repeat for the required number of rows.

Point protector

3 Starting with the second stitch, pass the stitches one by one over the first stitch. Slide the remaining stitch back onto the right needle and using the main needles, knit to the next bobble.

I-CORD BUTTON

For a bigger button, work a four or five stitch I-cord.

1 Knit 15¾in (40cm) of three stitch I-cord using a provisional cast-on (see pp. 45-46) and cast-off (see p. 50). Pin the left end to something secure with the I-cord stretching to the right. Make a counterclockwise loop that crosses back over itself to the right of the pin. This is loop A and it points away from you.

Loop A

2 Make another counterclockwise loop that lies sideways on, facing to the right, and which crosses over loop A except at the end, where it passes under the I-cord coming from the pin. This is loop B.

Loop A

Loop B

Over B, under A, over B, under A, through C so ends lie together

Loop A

Loop B

Loop C

3 Make another counterclockwise loop that faces toward you; this is loop C. The end of this loop has to be woven over and under loops A and B. It goes in over the first I-cord of loop B, then under the first I-cord of loop A, then over the second I-cord of loop B and then out under the second I-cord of loop A. Finally, bring this end toward you over all the I-cords, and thread it down through loop C.

4 Gently pull both ends to shape the button into a ball. Either unravel the ends of the cord and sew the yarn ends in to complete the button, or cast off and appliqué the I-cord ends to the garment for a decorative "frogging" effect.

Colorwork

You have many technique choices if you like adding colors to your knitting. The easiest method is to knit plain stockinette stitch using a multicolored yarn or a variegated yarn, which changes color along the strand. To add colors into the knitting yourself, you can work simple stripes, easy colorwork stitch patterns, or charted Fair Isle or intarsia motifs.

Simple stripes

Horizontal stripes are perfect for knitters who want to have fun with color without learning more advanced techniques. These examples show the variety of stripe widths, colors, and textures available. You can follow any plainly colored pattern and introduce stripes without affecting the gauge or shape of the knitting.

TWO-COLOR GARTER STITCH STRIPE

This stripe pattern is worked in garter stitch in two colors (A and B). To work the stripe, knit 2 rows in each color alternately, dropping the color not in use at the side of the work and picking it up when it is needed again.

TWO-COLOR KNIT AND PURL PINSTRIPE

Knit this stripe in two colors (A and B). Work 6 rows in stockinette stitch in A. Drop A at the side and knit 2 rows in B—the second of these rows creates a purl ridge on the right side. Repeat this sequence for the pinstripe effect. To avoid loose strands of B at the edge, wrap A around B at the start of every RS row.

FIVE-COLOR STOCKINETTE STITCH STRIPE

To work multiple stripes and carry the colors up the side, use a circular needle. Work back and forth in rows. If a yarn you need to pick up is at the opposite end, push all the stitches back to the other end of the circular needle and work the next row with the same side of the knitting facing as the last row.

TEXTURED STOCKINETTE STITCH STRIPE

This stripe is worked in a mohair yarn in two colors (A and B) and a smooth cotton yarn (C). The cotton yarn provides a good contrast in texture and sheen and highlights the fuzziness of the mohair.

PLAIN-COLOR DOMINO SQUARES

1 Cast on 21 stitches with the knit-on method (see p. 36). First row is a wrong side row. Slip first stitch knitwise, knit another 8 stitches and add a stitch marker. Knit the middle 3 stitches and put in another marker. Knit 8 more stitches, then purl the remaining stitch.

2 Slip first stitch knitwise, knit to first marker. (Move markers up as you knit.) S1 k2tog psso (see p. 79). Knit to end, purling the last stitch.

3 Slip first stitch knitwise, knit to last but one stitch, purl the last stitch. Right side rows, on which the s1 k2tog psso is worked on the center three stitches, are identified by the yarn tail being at the right.

4 Repeat steps 2 and 3 until you have one stitch left. Cut the yarn and pull the end through as normal, but not tightly so that it can be rethreaded when another square is knitted on.

NEATENING THE EDGES

When working two colored, even-row stripes, twist the yarns around each other every ½–¾in (1–2cm) up the side of the piece. Alternating the direction of the twist after each color change prevents the yarns from becoming tangled. Be careful not to pull them tightly or the edge will pucker. This technique may make a bulky seam if used with more than two colors.

STRIPED DOMINO SQUARES

1 Working as plain domino square, cast on 21 stitches. Knit the first row in the main color.

2 Continue as plain domino square, alternating two rows of contrast and main color as you work. To join in the contrast yarn see p. 62. Carry the yarns up the side as you work.

JOINING DOMINO SQUARES

1 With RS of original square facing and needle with remaining end stitch from last square in right hand, pick up and knit 10 stitches along the edge of the original square using yarn for new square (see p. 64). Pick up through the center of loops of edge stitches. ┄┄┄┄┄

2 Cast on another 10 stitches on left needle using knit-on method (see p. 36). Knit this square as for plain color domino knitting (see opposite). ┄┄

3 Continue to add squares, using different colored yarns as required. When combined with the following technique, no sewing is required at all.

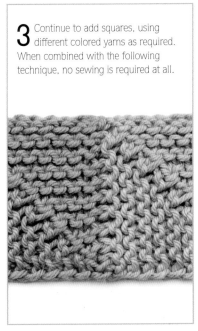

WEAVING IN ENDS DURING DOMINO KNITTING

1 On RS rows it is possible to weave in ends as you knit. Start with the lowest end, with the new color held in the right hand, and the old color over the left index finger.

2 Insert right needle into first left stitch, bring old color (on left finger) around front of right needle from right to left.

3 Lay new color between needles as normal and knit the stitch; as you pass the new color loop off the needle, allow the old color to slide to the right and over the tip of the right needle so that it does not catch in the new stitch. Knit one stitch without weaving the old color. ┄┄┄┄

4 Repeat steps 2 and 3 until the tail of the old color is woven in and then drop it for trimming later and complete the square. Trim it, leaving about ½in (1cm) of yarn to prevent it from unraveling on the right side.

Colorwork stitch patterns

Slip-stitch patterns are designed specially to use more than one color in the overall pattern but only ever use one color in a row. With this technique, geometric patterns are created by working some stitches in a row and slipping others. The pattern here is shown in two different colorways and is one of the easiest to work.

BOX SLIP-STITCH PATTERN

Follow this pattern to work the stitch and use the steps below as a guide.

Use three colors that contrast in tone:
A (a medium-toned color), B (a light-toned color), and C (a dark-toned color).

Note: Slip all slip stitches purlwise with the yarn on the WS of the work.

Using A, cast on a multiple of 4 stitches, plus 2 extra.

Row 1 (WS) (WS) Using A, P to end.

Row 2 (RS) (RS) Using B, K1, sl 1, *K2, sl 2; rep from * to last 3 sts, K2, sl 1, K1.

Row 3 Using B, P1, sl 1, *P2, sl 2; rep from * to last 3 sts, P2, sl 1, P1.

Row 4 Using A, K to end.

Row 5 Using C, P2, *sl 2, P2; rep from *.

Row 6 Using C, K2, *sl 2, K2; rep from *.

Rep rows 1–6 to form patt.

WORKING A BOX SLIP-STITCH PATTERN

1 This shows the middle of a pattern row 2 (RS row) of the pattern above. Two stitches have been slipped. On RS rows, slip the stitches with yarn held at the back. Do not pull the yarn too tightly on the following stitches.

Yarn B

Two slipped stitches

Right side

2 Row 4 of the pattern is worked entirely with yarn A and no stitches are slipped. The slipped stitches on the previous row and on the following row pull the stitches in A up and down to produce the box effect.

Yarn A

Right side

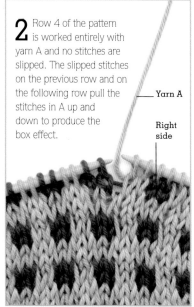

3 On WS rows of the check pattern, slip the stitches with yarn held at the front. The principle of all the slip-stitch patterns is the same—only one color is used in a row.

Yarn C

Two slipped stitches

Wrong side

Charted colorwork

The techniques for charted stockinette-stitch colorwork—Fair Isle and intarsia—open up a world of richly colored designs. In Fair Isle, a yarn color is carried across the wrong side of the work until it is required. In intarsia, a separate length of yarn is used for each color and the yarns are twisted together at the color change junctures.

FOLLOWING A COLORWORK CHART

The first step in understanding charted colorwork is to grasp how easy the charts are to follow. Rather than writing out how many stitches in which colors to work across a row, your knitting pattern provides a chart with the colors marked on it in symbols or in blocks of color.

If a pattern covers the whole garment back, front, and sleeve and cannot be repeated, a large chart is provided for each of these elements with all the stitches on it for the entire piece. Where a pattern is a simple repeat, the repeat alone is charted. Each square on a stockinette-stitch colorwork chart represents a stitch and each

horizontal row of squares represents a knitted row. You follow the chart from the bottom to the top, just as your knitting forms on the needles.

The key provided with the chart tells you which color to use for each stitch. All odd-numbered rows on a colorwork chart are usually right-side (knit) rows and are read from right to left. All even-numbered rows on a colorwork chart are usually wrong-side (purl) rows and are read from left to right. Always read your knitting pattern instructions carefully to make sure that the chart follows these general rules.

FAIR ISLE CHART

This example of a Fair Isle chart illustrates very clearly how easy it is to knit simple Fair Isle patterns. No more than two colors are used in a row, which makes it ideal for colorwork beginners. The color not in use is stranded across the back of the knitting until it is needed again.

To identify if a colorwork chart should be worked in the Fair Isle technique, check that both colors in a row are used across the entire row. If each color is used after every three or four stitches (as in this chart), use the stranding technique (see p. 98). If the colors are not used over a span of more than three or four stitches, use the weaving-in techniques (see pp. 98–101) so that the loose strands (called floats) don't become too long.

KEY
☐ = background color
⦿ = motif color

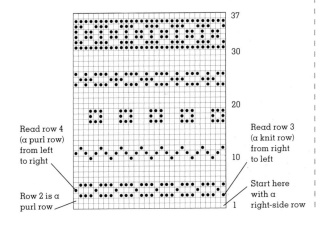

Read row 4 (a purl row) from left to right

Row 2 is a purl row

Read row 3 (a knit row) from right to left

Start here with a right-side row

INTARSIA CHART

This heart is an example of a simple intarsia colorwork chart. Each color on the chart is represented by a different symbol. The blank square (the background) also represents a color.

You can tell that a charted design should be worked in the intarsia technique if a color appears only in a section of a row and is not needed across the entire row. Use a separate long length of yarn, or yarn on a bobbin, for each area of color in intarsia knitting (including separated background areas). Twist the colors where they meet (see p. 104).

KEY
☐ = background color   ⦿ = motif color 2
⦿ = motif color 1   ⊠ = motif color 3

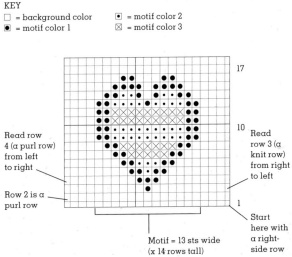

Read row 4 (a purl row) from left to right

Row 2 is a purl row

Read row 3 (a knit row) from right to left

Start here with a right-side row

Motif = 13 sts wide (x 14 rows tall)

Fair Isle method

This is where two or more colors are used in a row of knitting—traditionally, the colors would make small repeating patterns in stockinette stitch. The nonworking yarn is stranded along the wrong side, or may be woven into the back to keep it from catching.

FAIR ISLE STRANDING TECHNIQUE

1 On the knit rows, knit the stitches in the first color, then drop it at the back and knit the stitches in the second color. Strand the color not in use loosely across the back of the work until required.

2 Work the purl rows in the same way, but strand the color not in use across the front (wrong side). Keep one color on top and the other underneath so they do not twist around each other.

3 The trick to Fair Isle knitting is to learn to keep the gauge even, as shown here. The stranding should not be too loose or too tight. With continued practice knitting the correct gauge will become automatic.

Holding the yarns

These techniques for holding the yarns will speed up your work and produce more even results. To maintain consistent weight fabric, always carry both yarns to the edge even if no stitch is required there, and twist them before starting the next row.

HOLDING ONE YARN IN EACH HAND

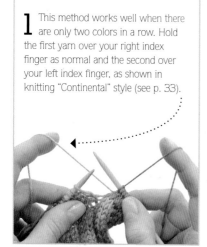

1 This method works well when there are only two colors in a row. Hold the first yarn over your right index finger as normal and the second over your left index finger, as shown in knitting "Continental" style (see p. 33).

2 Knit the first color stitches as usual. When you reach the second color stitches keep the first color over your right index finger. Insert the right needle into next stitch as if to knit. With your left index finger, lay the second color forward between the needles from left to right.

3 Pull the new knit loop through as usual, keeping both yarns over the correct index finger. On a purl row, follow the instructions for alternative "Continental" purl stitch (see p. 34) to work the color over your left index finger.

BOTH YARNS IN RIGHT HAND

Place one color over your right index finger, and one over your middle finger. Knit as normal, throwing the second color with your middle finger. This method allows you the flexibility of potentially adding a third color over your ring finger.

BOTH YARNS IN LEFT HAND

This is ideal for those who knit Continental style. Hold the first yarn over the index finger, and the second over the middle finger of your left hand. Throw the yarns with their respective fingers for knit and purl as shown on p. 34.

Techniques for weaving

When strands (or floats, as they are also known) are longer than three or four stitches, they may catch on fingers or rings. To prevent this, weave the nonworking yarn into the back of the knitting by taking the weaving yarn over and under the working yarn. This can be done on every other stitch, which makes a denser fabric, or whenever a float is longer than three stitches, in which case weave into occasional stitches.

WEAVING LEFT YARN, KNIT OR PURL

1 This method uses one yarn in each hand. Keep left yarn and finger below and to the left of needles when not weaving it in. Lift weaving yarn up, insert right needle through stitch to either knit or purl and underneath weaving yarn. Make stitch with main yarn, slipping weaving yarn over needle without catching in stitch.

2 Knit or purl the stitch, catching floating yarn in back of the fabric. Knit the next stitch without weaving in left yarn, by dropping left finger to back so the yarn lies below the needles before making the stitch. Weave in as necessary to prevent long floats.

Weaving yarn (left)

Working yarn (right)

WEAVING RIGHT YARN, KNIT STITCH

1 This method uses one yarn in each hand. Keep right yarn above and to the right of the needles when not weaving it in. To weave, insert right needle into stitch. Wind right yarn around needle as to knit, throw left yarn as usual to knit. . .

2 Return right yarn back along its route to original position and knit the stitch. Knit the next stitch without wrapping the right yarn. Weave in as necessary to prevent long floats.

Working yarn (left)

Weaving yarn (right)

WEAVING RIGHT YARN, PURL STITCH

1 This method uses one yarn in each hand. On a purl stitch, keeping the left index finger and yarn below the needles, Wind the right yarn under the right needle. Throw left yarn as usual to purl, return right yarn back along its route to original position and purl the stitch. Work the next stitch without weaving the right yarn. Weave in as necessary to prevent long floats.

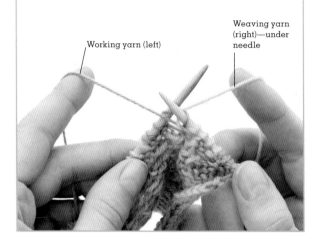

Working yarn (left)

Weaving yarn (right)—under needle

WEAVING INDEX FINGER YARN

1 Holding both yarns in right hand, insert right needle into stitch, wind both yarns around needle as if to knit.

2 Return index finger yarn to its original position. Knit the stitch with the remaining yarn. Keep weaving yarn above the needles when not weaving. Knit the next stitch without weaving the index finger yarn in. Weave in as necessary to prevent long floats.

Weaving yarn

Working yarn

[RIGHT HAND] WEAVING MIDDLE FINGER YARN WHILE KNITTING OR PURLING A STITCH

1 Hold both yarns in right hand. Keep middle finger yarn above work when not weaving in. To knit or purl, insert right needle into stitch. Bring middle finger yarn above index finger yarn, across front of both needles to the left.

2 Holding yarn in place to the left of the needles, take it around to the right behind the needles.

Catch middle finger yarn with left thumb and/or index finger

Hold both yarns in right hand

3 Throw the index finger yarn as if to knit or purl, then return middle finger yarn back along its route to its original position at right back of work. Work next stitch without weaving, temporarily lowering middle finger so index finger yarn wraps around middle finger yarn. Weave in as necessary to prevent long floats.

Working yarn (index)

[LEFT HAND] WEAVING INDEX FINGER YARN WHILE KNITTING OR PURLING A STITCH

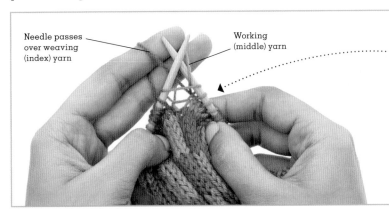

Needle passes over weaving (index) yarn

Working (middle) yarn

1 Hold both yarns in left hand. Keep index finger yarn above work when not weaving in. To weave in, insert right needle into stitch making sure the needle goes over index finger yarn (drop index finger). Lay middle finger yarn over needle to work stitch as normal.

2 Draw yarn through as normal, taking care not to catch the index finger yarn into the stitch. Raise index finger yarn again and work next stitch without weaving. Weave in as necessary to prevent long floats.

HOLDING BOTH YARNS IN LEFT HAND—WEAVING THE MIDDLE FINGER YARN

1 Here, the middle finger yarn is more awkward to weave than that on the index finger. Keep the middle finger below the work when not weaving. Insert the right needle into stitch, making sure it passes under both yarns.

2 Bring the tip back over the middle finger (weaving) yarn and catch the index finger yarn. Draw it under the middle finger yarn to make a new stitch. Work next stitch without weaving. Weave to prevent long floats.

KNIT AND PURL FAIR ISLE

1 At the position where a purl stitch is to be introduced, bring the working yarn to the front and purl the required number of stitches. Take the yarn to the back and continue the pattern in knit stitch. Strand the yarns at the back of the knitting.

2 If you wish to maintain clear color transitions, knit the first row of a new color, purl the middle rows, and knit the row immediately before a color change.

GARTER STITCH FAIR ISLE

1 Work every row of pattern twice, knitting all rows. At the end of every row, wrap the yarns around each other to secure them.

2 Knit the first (RS) row, stranding on the back. Start the second (WS) row with the nonworking yarn at the front, and the working one at the back.

3 When it is time to change color, swap the yarn positions from front to back, and continue, stranding the nonworking yarn at the front (WS) of the work.

4 For smooth transition when changing or finishing a color, do so on the first of the two row pattern (RS) row.

TEA-COZY STITCH

1 Twist yarns at the start of each row. Pull stranding yarn gently throughout to slightly gather the knitting. Knit eight stitches in the first color, stranding second yarn at back. Swap yarns, knit eight stitches in second color stranding first yarn at back. Repeat along the row.

Wrong side of knitting

2 Next row. First color to back, second to front, knit first eight stitches. First color to front, second to back, knit eight stitches in second color. Repeat along row, swapping yarns from front to back so that both yarns strand on the front. Repeat steps 1 and 2.

TWO STRAND LAYING-IN

1 Work stockinette stitch in main yarn, all yarns at back. When decorative yarns are required on knit side, bring to front between needles. Work the number of stitches required in main yarn. Decorative yarns to back. Work in main yarn.

2 Do not twist main and decorative yarns when they are moved from front to back.

3 On a purl row, all yarns to front. When decorative yarns are required to lie on the knit side, take back between needles and work number of stitches required in main yarn. Decorative yarns to front between needles. Work in main yarn.

KNIT WEAVE

Shows on reverse of stockinette stitch. Always work one plain stitch between weaves. Twist the yarns at start of every row. Weaving yarn lies alternately over and under main yarn.

1 On a K row. Both yarns at back, insert needle to knit. Lay weaving yarn right to left between needles. Knit with main yarn, do not catch weaving yarn.

2 On a P row. Both yarns at front, weaving yarn below main yarn between weaves. Insert needle to purl, lay weaving yarn right to left between needles. Purl with main yarn.

Intarsia

Here each yarn is worked separately and no strands are carried along the back. Each area of color in a row must have its own small ball of yarn. Cut short lengths from the main balls and wind onto bobbins to prevent tangles.

INTARSIA TECHNIQUE

Right-slant color change: To avoid holes, twist the colors around each other only on the knit rows.

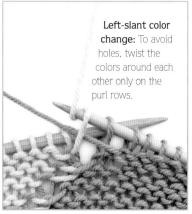

Left-slant color change: To avoid holes, twist the colors around each other only on the purl rows.

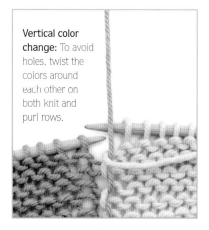

Vertical color change: To avoid holes, twist the colors around each other on both knit and purl rows.

TWO-COLOR CABLES

1 Wind sufficient small balls for intarsia. Work two vertical stripes of A with three-stitch vertical stripes in B and C in between (this is the six-stitch cable). Stop after the purl row before the first crossover.

2 Knit A to cable position. Slip the three C stitches off the left needle onto a cable needle and put to the back.

3 Bring B yarn under A yarn (this is the twist) and take behind stitches on cable needle. Knit the three B stitches off the left and onto the right needle.

4 With C, and without twisting the yarn, knit the three C stitches off the cable needle and onto the right needle.

5 Twist A under C and knit stitches between cables. On the next (purl) row, when twisting B and A the yarns will stretch diagonally at rear of crossover. Do not pull too tightly.

6 Work 7 rows of stripes to next crossover row. Work crossover as steps 2–5, reversing C and B.

Textural and color effects

With a simple stockinette and garter stitch base, prettily knotted, shaded, pulled, and gathered effects can be achieved. Loop stitch variations offer versatile decorative edging possibilities and careful yarn color and type choices will also enhance these techniques.

Working into lower stitches

The following techniques add texture to the knitted surface. Combinations of textural and open lacelike knitting can be produced by dropping and unraveling stitches, while dip stitch adds color. Pull up stitch creates three-dimensional effects.

BRIOCHE RIB

1 Insert right tip from front to back into the center of the stitch immediately below the next stitch to be taken off the left needle.

2 Wrap yarn around the tip of the needle at the back.

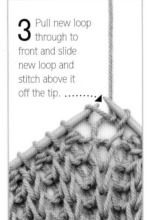

3 Pull new loop through to front and slide new loop and stitch above it off the tip.

4 Knit the next stitch. Repeat steps 1–3 for each double stitch. A plain stitch is always worked between each double.

DROPPING AND UNRAVELING STITCHES AND ROWS

1 When you reach the desired position, drop the stitch that you wish to unravel and pull on it until it unravels to the desired position.

2 Making sure you put the needle beneath the unraveled strands, insert the right needle into the last stitch below that has not unraveled.

3 Knit the loose strands and the stitch together. Knit the next stitch before dropping another stitch.

PULL UP STITCH

1 Work stockinette stitch to position of pull up stitch, on a purl row. Reach right needle down purl side and insert tip into top loop of stitch to be pulled up.

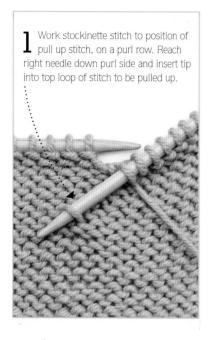

2 Slip the stitch knitwise onto the left needle and purl together with the following stitch on the needle. Space as required along row. ⋯⋯⋯

3 When the piece is completed the pull up stitch creates a tucked, raised effect.

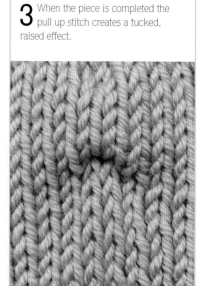

LONG STITCH

Long stitch can be vertical or angled across the front or reverse of knitting, and worked in main color for texture or contrast for a color effect.

1 Knit to where the effect is to occur. Reach the right needle tip down a number of rows and insert tip through a stitch (or the space between two stitches).

Needle insertion positions

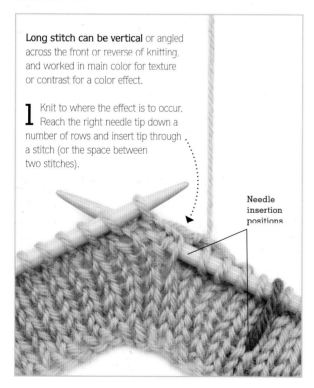

2 Holding second yarn at back, catch "dip" yarn with needle and pull through to front. Pull enough through, and make the rear strands loose enough so that the main fabric is not distorted. On the next row, knit or purl the "dip" stitch together with the following stitch. Repeat steps 1 and 2 whenever a long stitch is required.

Decorative stitches

With a few uncomplicated moves, elaborate looking effects are possible. Picot point chains can be worked into filet lacelike fabrics or make delicate trims. Shadow knitting might look complicated, but it is a simple technique that uses only knit and purl stitches. Just remember that each row of the original pattern represents four rows of stitches in your final piece of knitting.

THREE-INTO-THREE STITCH

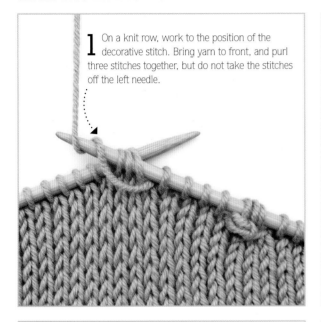

1 On a knit row, work to the position of the decorative stitch. Bring yarn to front, and purl three stitches together, but do not take the stitches off the left needle.

2 Yarn to back, knit into the three stitches that are still on the left needle, but do not take the stitches off the left needle.

3 Yarn to front, purl into the same three stitches again, then slide the three stitches off the left needle. Yarn to back and knit any intervening stitches in pattern.

4 The next row is usually a plain row, either knit or purl depending on your overall pattern.

5 The three-into-three stitch forms a raised bobble on the surface of the knitting, creating a pattern when worked regularly.

WRAPPED CLUSTERS

1 At the position of the cluster, slip the last five stitches on the right needle all together without twisting onto a cable needle.

2 Wrap the yarn in a counterclockwise direction around the stitches taking it underneath the cable needle. Wrap yarn six times, pulling it tight if you want the cluster to gather the stitches.

3 Slip the cable needle stitches straight back onto the right needle. Work row as normal to next cluster.

PICOT CHAIN

1 Make a slip knot on the left needle.

2 Knit-on cast-on (see p. 36) two more stitches. Knitwise cast off (see p. 50) two stitches so there is one stitch remaining on right needle.

3 Slip the stitch onto the left needle without twisting. Repeat step 2 to make a chain of the required length.

4 To make flower circles, work a five picot chain and then insert the needle into the base of the first picot, draw the loop through and cast off the last stitch.

KNITTED SMOCKING

1 Cast on a multiple of eight stitches plus three, and work a purl three, knit one rib. This is a right side row. Knit an even number of rows in rib until the position of the first smocking is reached.

2 Work eight stitches of the rib. Slip last five stitches on right needle together onto a cable needle. Bring smocking yarn from back to front between right needle and cable needle leaving a 4in (10cm) tail at back. Wind this yarn twice clockwise around stitches on cable needle, leaving it at back of work.

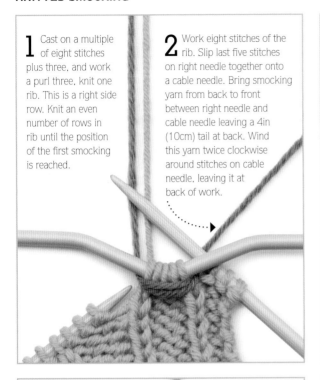

3 Slip stitches together off cable needle back onto right needle. Repeat steps 2 and 3 across row, stranding smocking yarn across back of work and cutting with a 4in (10cm) tail at the end.

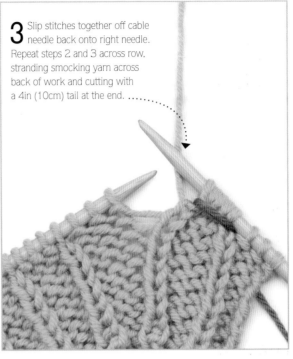

4 Work three rows of rib and then repeat steps 2 and 3 but work the first twelve stitches before introducing smocking yarn.

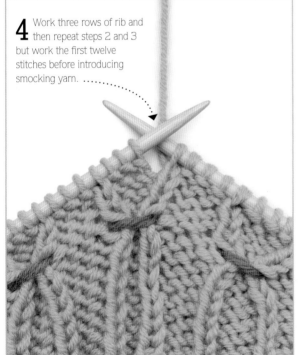

5 Continue to work smocking alternating the start of eight or twelve stitches with three rows between. When complete, secure the ends of smocking yarn up one edge. Gently draw up each row of smocking, easing ribs together until finally securing the smocking yarn at the other edge.

SHADOW KNITTING

1 The design chart shows the finished effect.

2 This chart has to be "exploded," and drawn on a knitting chart that is four times as long as the original.

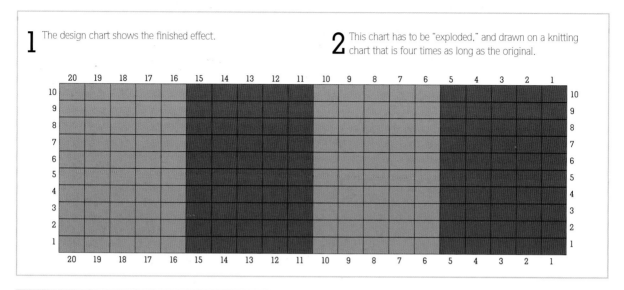

3 The first row of the exploded chart is always left blank. On the second row, draw the main (pink) stitches from row 1 of the original chart.

4 Leave three rows blank, then draw the main (pink) stitches from row 2 of the original chart; continue in this manner to the final row (row 10).

5 Go back to the beginning of the exploded chart, and on the middle row of the three blank rows, draw the contrast (gray) stitches from row 1 of the original chart. Continue up the exploded chart matching original chart stitches to the middle of the blank rows.

6 Annotate the chart in your own way to show purl and knit stitches. Color every two rows in alternating colors, starting with two rows of main color. This example shows purl stitches as white to help read the chart, but work them in whichever color stripe they fall in.

KEY

—	Purl
I	Knit
■	Main color A
■	Contrast color B

7 Cast on 20 stitches and, working from chart, knit the first row in color A. Work second row in A, purling the white squares and knitting the colored ones.

8 Change to color B, knit one plain row and then work as row 4 of chart, purling the blank squares and knitting the colored ones. Repeat the color sequence of two rows of each color as you follow the chart upward.

Structural effects

Structural knitting techniques are challenging and satisfying to work, and can be used in combination with varied colors and textural yarns. Entrelac squares offer scope for color choices while pleats, gathering, and blousing can add style details to garments. Tubular knitting is an interesting technique and, alongside bias knitting, may inspire new ideas.

Entrelac

Here, knitted squares create a diagonal basketweave effect. Squares can be worked in stockinette stitch, garter stitch, cables, or textural stitches. Each square has twice as many rows as stitches and alternating series of squares are worked in opposite directions. All the stitches for one series are on the needle at the same time, although the squares are worked individually. A line of short row triangles at the start, finish, and each side, create straight edges.

1 This example makes three eight-stitch squares. In color A, loosely cast on 24 stitches using knit-on method (see p. 36). Knit 2 stitches and turn work. Purl one stitch, slip one purlwise, turn. This slip stitch makes picking up in step 7 easier.

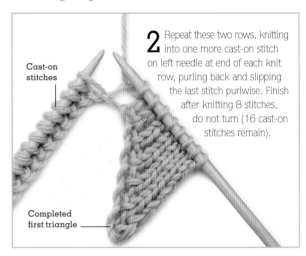

2 Repeat these two rows, knitting into one more cast-on stitch on left needle at end of each knit row, purling back and slipping the last stitch purlwise. Finish after knitting 8 stitches, do not turn (16 cast-on stitches remain).

Cast-on stitches

Completed first triangle

3 Work the next triangle as in steps 1 and 2 over the following 8 stitches, and the third triangle over the final 8 stitches. There are now three triangles on the needle.

4 Left side triangle. WS facing, join in color B and purl 2 stitches, turn, knit 2, turn. Purl into front and back of edge stitch (see p. 70), this shapes the edge. Purl the last stitch in color B together with the first stitch in color A (p2tog, see p. 77) on the right needle.

P2tog

5 Repeat step 4, purling one more stitch for each repeat and knitting back to the edge each time. Stop after purling into front and back, purling 5 and purling color B and color A together. Do not turn work. Leave this completed edge triangle on the right needle. ....

6 To work squares. WS facing, yarn at front. Insert right needle from back to front into edge stitches and pick up and purl 8 stitches evenly along the free edge of first triangle. ....

7 Turn work and knit 7 stitches, slip one purlwise, turn work. Purl 7, then purl the last stitch in color B together with the first stitch in color A (p2tog, see p. 77) on the right needle. This joins the new square to the old triangle. Turn work.

8 Repeat step 7 seven more times, but do not turn work after last row, all stitches of first square are now on left needle. Work next square as steps 6–8.

9 To work right edge triangle. WS facing, pick up edge as step 6. Work every knit row, slipping the end stitch purlwise. P2tog at the end of all but the first purl row. One stitch remains.

Right edge triangle

Base triangle

10 To work right edge square. Join in color A. With RS facing, slip first stitch onto right needle. Pick up and knit 7 stitches along the edge of right-hand square (8 stitches on needle). Purl 7, slip 1 purlwise, turn.

11 Knit 7. Work ssk with next 2 stitches (one of each color). Repeat last two rows to end of join. Work steps 10 (omit slip, pick up 8 sts instead) and 11 for all squares. Steps 4–11 make one complete pattern repeat.

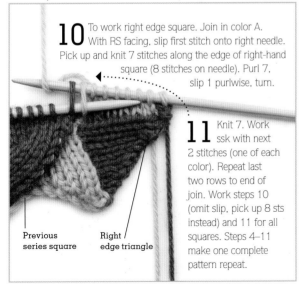

Previous series square

Right edge triangle

12 Work finished triangles (these follow a series with edge triangles—see steps 4–9). In appropriate color, work as step 10, purling 8 in final instruction. Turn. Knit 7, work an ssk as in step 11. Turn, purl 6, p2tog at end to create flat top edge. Turn, knit 6 and ssk as before.

13 Continue working ssk and p2tog each time until triangle completed. Repeat for all triangles. Pull final stitch through itself to finish.

Structural effects **113**

Pleats

To make a pattern for pleats, fold a sheet of squared paper alternately away from and toward you along lines at 10 and 5 square intervals. Each square represents a stitch. Use the pattern to count the stitches required to make the visible face, underside, and turn-back of each pleat. Add one stitch at each fold—slipped on right side, purled on wrong side rows, or purled every row. Use the same method for all folds.

KNITTING PLEATS

Turn back   Under side   Visible face

1 This example creates two left-facing 5-stitch pleats. Cast on 44 stitches (this includes an extra 4 stitches for fold lines).

2 Add markers as you work. First row: k10, p1, k5, p1, k10, p1, k5, p1, k10.

First stitch of visible face of pleat

3 Purl one complete row. Repeat steps 2 and 3 to required length, finishing after a purl row.

4 When pleats completed, cast off 4 stitches knitwise (see p. 50). Slip the next 5 stitches purlwise (including fold stitch) onto a double-pointed needle (dpn). Slip the next 6 stitches purlwise (including the fold stitch) onto another dpn. Turn the needles to fold the pleat.

Rear dpn   Left needle

5 Slip one stitch from rear dpn to right needle. Knit the first stitch on the left needle onto the right needle and pass both stitches on right needle over the first one and needle tip, one by one.

6 Slip one stitch from front dpn and one from rear dpn onto right needle. Knit the first stitch on the left needle and pass the 3 stitches over one by one. Repeat this step until all pleats are cast off. ....

Left needle

Double-pointed needles

7 Cast off remaining stitches as normal.

Gathering and blousing

Gathering removes multiple stitches evenly along a row, and blousing (also called doubling) adds stitches in the same manner. Another form of gathering can be created by working multiple rows of rib on smaller needles preceded and followed by non-rib knitting. Blousing can be used very effectively after a cuff rib, giving fullness to a sleeve.

GATHERING

1 To calculate even gathering, decide how many stitches are to be removed, and divide the stitches on the needle by this number. For example, if you cast on 30 stitches and wish to remove 10 stitches evenly, the sum is 30 ÷ 10 = 3. Therefore, one stitch must be decreased in every three stitches. To do this, knit one stitch, then knit two stitches together (k2tog). Repeat along the row.

2 To make a fuller gather, try k2tog all across the row, or knit 3 stitches together or even work two consecutive k2tog, p2tog rows. To create a gathered edge, knit two or more stitches together as you cast off.

BLOUSING

1 To calculate blousing, do the same addition as for gathering (above), but remember that blousing adds stitches. If the answer is three, then three stitches must be made out of every one stitch. To do this, knit into front, back, and front again of each stitch.

2 To use both blousing and gathering to work a horizontal ruffle, knit one row, knitting into front and back, and the next row purling into front and back of each stitch. Knit between 16 and 20 rows in stockinette stitch. Knit one row k2tog across row, and then p2tog across next row. Continue in stockinette stitch.

Bias knitting

This method creates diagonal-shaped pieces, sloping left or right. Chevron knitting (see p. 199) is created by working opposing bias panels in one piece. Increasing into lower rows or working increases tightly can force bias knitting to curve attractively.

BIAS KNITTING—STRAIGHT AND CURVED

1 Cast on 20 stitches. At the start of the first knit row, slip first and second stitch one by one onto right needle, insert left needle into front and knit them together (ssk, see p. 78). Knit row to one before the end stitch, knit into front and back of edge stitch. Purl one row. Repeat knit row. This piece of knitting will slant to the left.

2 To slant to the right, knit into front and back of first stitch, knit to two from end and k2tog.

3 To add neat, decorative edges slanting to the left, knit two stitches, then work the ssk decrease, knit to three stitches from end and work a left lifted increase (see p. 81) by knitting into left front of stitch two rows below just completed stitch. Knit to end.

Short rows

Rows of knitting do not necessarily have to be knitted end to end. Knitting short rows, or "partial knitting," involves knitting two rows across some of the stitches, thereby adding rows in only one part of the fabric. It is popular for creating smooth edges in shoulder shaping, curving hems, making darts, and turning sock heels. It is most commonly used on stockinette stitch.

Preventing holes

In most shaping applications a concealed turn is required and there are three ways to work this: the "wrap" or "tie" (easiest and neat); the "over" (loosest); and the "catch" (neatest). Garter stitch, as shown in the 3-D ball, does not require wrapping.

WRAP OR TIE TO CLOSE HOLES

1 On a knit row: at turn position, slip next stitch purlwise onto right needle (see p. 65), yarn to front. Return slip stitch to left needle, yarn back. Turn and purl short row. Repeat wrap at each mid-row turn.

2 On a purl row: at turn, slip next stitch purlwise, yarn to back. Slip stitch back, yarn to front. Turn and work knit short row. Repeat wrap at each mid-row turn.

3 When working across all stitches on completion of short row: at wrap, insert right needle up through front (knit) or back (purl) of wrap. Work wrap together with next stitch.

OVER TO CLOSE HOLES

1 Knit or purl to turn position. Turn. Bring yarn to other side of work and bring yarn over needle (without moving yarn to back or front beforehand, so yarn does not go completely around needle). Work short row.

2 When knitting across all stitches on completion of short row, knit yarn-over and next stitch together.

3 When purling across all stitches on completion of short row, drop yarn over and slip next stitch purlwise. Insert left needle downward into dropped yarn, pick it up, and purl together with next stitch.

CATCH TO CLOSE HOLES

1 On either knit or purl rows, work a short row. Turn work, slip first stitch purlwise (see p. 65), and work back along short row.

2 When knitting a completion row (work is temporarily reversed, to make this step easier), insert right needle down through strand between first and second stitches on left needle as shown. Lift onto left needle.

Insert right needle one row below row just worked

Left needle

3 Turn work again and knit picked up loop together with next stitch on left needle.

4 Iff completion row is purl, insert left needle upward through the strand between the first and second two rows below right needle. Stretch this loop, then drop it. Slip next stitch from left to right needle. Pick up dropped loop again with left needle. Return slipped stitch to left needle. Purl these two together.

Left needle

Right needle

SHAPING: ADAPTING A CAST-OFF SHOULDER TO SHORT ROW SHAPING

1 This example adapts an existing left shoulder shaping worked in stockinette stitch. The shoulder is 24 stitches wide and the original instruction is to cast off 8 stitches every alternate row. These cast-offs can be substituted by working short rows with 8 less stitches every alternate row.

2 Cast on 24 stitches and work to the shoulder shaping. Ignore the first cast-off instruction, knitting a complete row instead. Turn work.

3 Purl to 8 stitches from the end and work a wrap (slip next stitch purlwise, yarn back, return slip stitch, yarn forward, see opposite). Turn and knit to end.

4 Purl to 16 stitches from the end, work wrap and turn. Knit to end (8 stitches on needle).

5 Purl across all the stitches, picking up wraps by slipping them onto left needle and purling together with next stitch (see p. 117). Either cast off all stitches, or put them onto a stitch holder for grafting later.

SHORT ROW CIRCULAR MEDALLION

This example is in garter stitch, but medallions can be knitted in other stitches. There is no need to pick up the wraps in garter stitch.

1 Cast on 16 stitches in color A with a provisional cast-on (see p. 45).

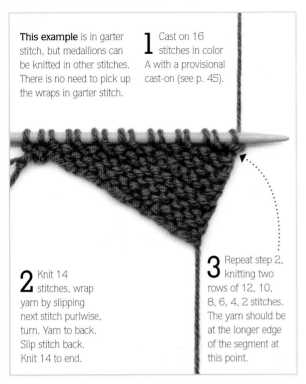

2 Knit 14 stitches, wrap yarn by slipping next stitch purlwise, turn. Yarn to back. Slip stitch back. Knit 14 to end.

3 Repeat step 2, knitting two rows of 12, 10, 8, 6, 4, 2 stitches. The yarn should be at the longer edge of the segment at this point.

4 Turn work and knit 14 stitches. Yarn to front. Slip last two stitches on left needle purlwise onto right needle. Cut color A yarn with a 4in (10cm) tail (yarn is partway along a row). One segment of the circle is completed.

5 Hold the needle with stitches in the left hand, change to color B, knit 16 stitches. Then repeat steps 2–5 in B, swapping to color A at step 5.

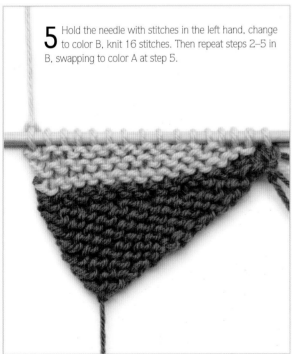

6 Work 8 segments, alternating colors A and B. Finish by placing stitches on a holder (see p. 50) after step 5 on the final segment. Graft (see p. 152) the seam and sew in the yarn ends to complete.

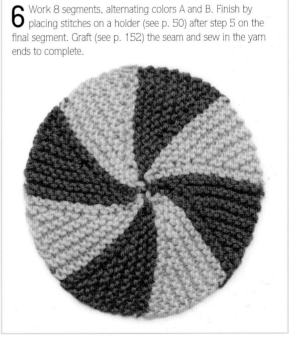

Ruffles

By working a straight band vertically at the same time as working short rows, ruffles can be built up. The fullness of the ruffle is dictated by the number of times the short rows are worked compared to the rows of the vertical band. Varying the stitch, as shown in edge ruffles, can add extra effect to the finished ruffle.

SHORT ROW EDGE RUFFLES

1 Working over 20 stitches, purl 14, work a wrap (see p. 117) turn and knit 14 back to edge.

2 Repeat step 1 twice.

— Garter-stitch edge

3 Purl 13 stitches and at position of wraps, insert right needle into back of wraps from underneath and slip all onto left needle. Purl wraps together with the next stitch. Purl to end. This step is important, since it adds fullness to the finished ruffle.

4 Purl 6, knit 14 stitches. Repeat steps 1–4 until you have the required length of garter-stitch straight edge.

VERTICAL RUFFLES INSET INTO FABRIC

1 This example uses 24 stitches. The ruffle is worked over the middle 8 stitches. Knit 16, wrap (see p. 117), and turn.

2 Purl 8 stitches, wrap, and turn.

3 Knit 8 stitches, wrap, and turn. Repeat step 2.

4 Knit 16 stitches, picking up wraps (see p. 117).

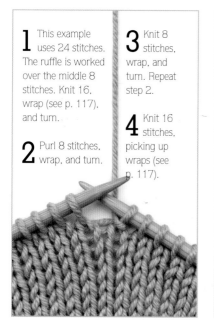

5 Purl 24 doing pick up on other side of ruffle, as in step 4. This completes two rows of main fabric and four rows of the inset ruffle.

6 Repeat from knit instruction in step 1 to end of step 5 for required number of side panel rows. Group vertically for greater effect.

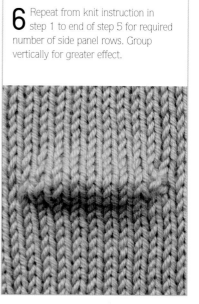

3-D knitting

Planned use of short rows can make your knitting take 3-D form. Peaks created in this way can be left open or sewn together at the base. Before joining, these can be padded to create a closed decorative "pocket." Ungraduated short row flaps can also be sewn up, padded, and joined. Complete 3-D shapes can also be worked.

SHORT ROW BALL

This example is in garter stitch and there is no wrapping included. If wrapping is required, follow the method shown in short row circular medallion (see p. 119).

1 Cast on 20 stitches in color A.

15 stitches completed

2 Knit 19 stitches, turn work, bring yarn to back. Repeat this step, knitting one less stitch on each row until 15 stitches have been knitted. Turn work, bring yarn to back.

Color A

3 Knit 13 stitches, turn work, yarn to back. Repeat this step knitting 11 stitches.

4 Knit 7 stitches, turn work, yarn to back. Repeat this step knitting 5 stitches.

5 Knit 4 stitches, yarn to front. Slip all remaining stitches (9) on left needle purlwise onto right needle. Cut yarn with 4in (10cm) tail.

8 more stitches to slip

Color B

Color A

6 Repeat steps 2–5 in color B.

7 Work 8 segments in alternate colors to complete ball. Cast off or work a provisional cast-off. Sew in mid-row ends and gently pull top and bottom threads to neaten ends. Stuff with suitable material and either sew together with mattress stitch (see p. 149), or graft provisional open stitches to cast-on edge.

SHORT ROW PEAKS

1 Decide the width of the peak, for this example it is 9 stitches and there are 8 stitches on both sides of it (25 stitches on needle). At position of peak, knit 17 stitches, turn.

2 Purl 9 stitches, turn.

3 Knit 8 stitches, turn. Including a turn after each row, purl 7, knit 6, purl 5, knit 4, purl 3, knit 2, purl 1.

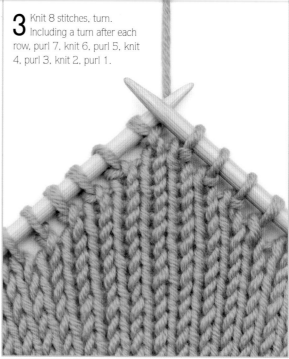

4 Knit 2, turn. Increasing in the reverse order to step 3 and turning at end of each row, work until the last row completed is purl 9 stitches. Turn.

5 Knit 17 stitches, turn, and purl 25 stitches. There may be small "steps" visible along the edge of the peak, this is part of the short row effect.

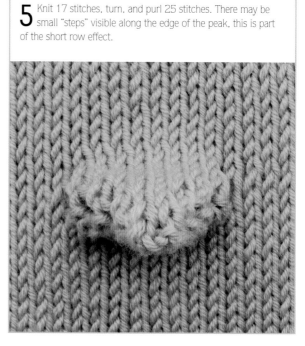

Circular knitting

Circular knitting, or knitting in the round, is worked on a circular needle or with a set of four or five double-pointed needles. With the right side always facing, the knitting is worked around and around to form a tube, or a flat shape (a medallion). A circular needle is easy to master, while working with double-pointed needles is best suited to knitters with intermediate skills.

Knitting tubes

For those who don't enjoy stitching seams, knitting seamless tubes is a real plus. Large tubes can be worked on long circular needles, for example, for the body of a sweater or a bag. Short circular needles are used for seamless neckbands and armhole bands, and hats. Double-pointed needles are used for smaller items such as mittens and socks.

WORKING WITH A CIRCULAR KNITTING NEEDLE

1 Cast on the required number of stitches. Ensure that the stitches are untwisted and they all face inward, then slip a stitch marker onto the end of the right needle to mark the beginning of the round.

Stitch marker

2 Hold the needle ends in your hands and bring the right needle up to the left needle to work the first stitch. Knit around and around on the stitches. When the stitch marker is reached, slip it from the left needle to the right needle.

Knit first stitch of first round tightly

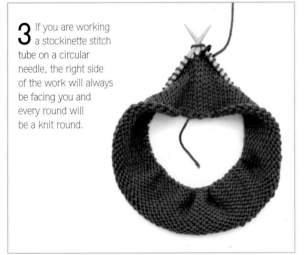

3 If you are working a stockinette stitch tube on a circular needle, the right side of the work will always be facing you and every round will be a knit round.

JOINING THE CIRCLE OF STITCHES

This is a neat way of closing the circle in circular knitting.

1 Cast on required number of stitches, plus one stitch.

2 Slip the first cast-on stitch onto the right needle next to last cast-on stitch. Place the join marker after this stitch.

3 Knit the round, and when you reach the end, knit the last two stitches before the marker together (this will be the first cast-on stitch and the extra stitch).

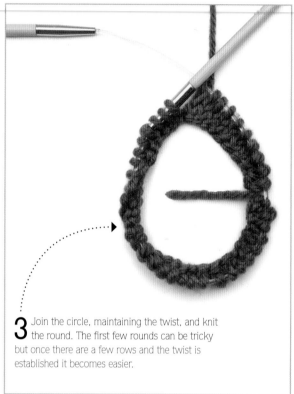

1 Using a long-tail cast-on (see p. 39) cast on enough stitches to work a circle on a short circular needle. Knit the first round but stop before joining the circle.

2 Deliberately twist the stitches around the wire so that there is one clear twist visible, but the end stitches are facing each other with the loops facing inward.

3 Join the circle, maintaining the twist, and knit the round. The first few rounds can be tricky but once there are a few rows and the twist is established it becomes easier.

5 Continue until the loop is as deep as required. Cast off. A deep mobius loop makes a great hair band.

4 If working on a long needle using the Magic Loop technique (shown here at the point when the cable has been pulled to divide the stitches), moving the twist to the stitches on the right of the needle for the first few rounds makes them easier to work.

KNITTING TWO TUBULAR ITEMS AT ONCE ON TWO CIRCULAR NEEDLES

This technique makes working pairs of tubular knitting, such as socks and gloves, seem quicker. Before you start, designate your needles A and B, and make a note of which is which.

1 Cast the stitches for tube 1 onto needle A using long-tail cast-on (see p. 39). Slide to opposite end. Divide stitches equally by slipping them purlwise onto needle B.

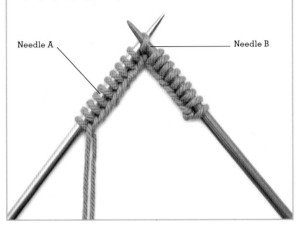

Needle A　　　　　Needle B

2 Push all the stitches at once to the other end of both needles.

3 Close the round by using a blunt-ended yarn needle to pass the short thread through the stitch by the long tail, and tying both ends in a tight knot. .....

Needle A _____　_____ Needle B

4 Cast on tube 2 with the second ball of yarn as step 1. Using the empty end of needle B, divide them onto needle A, and close the round as before.

5 Slide tube 2 (with working end away from needle tips) onto the cables. Place a marker on each tube at the first stitch by the working yarn. This marks the start of each round.

6 Lay the needles parallel and .... check that both your working ends of yarn face in the same direction, one being at the tips of the needles and one being halfway along on the cable.

Put point protector on needle A

Tube 1 _____

Needle B _____

Needle A _____

Tube 2 _____

7 Hold both needles in your left hand, needle A (with the protector) should be slightly behind B. The working yarn should hang between both needles so that it is in the correct position and does not make an extra stitch. The second yarn should lie over and behind the needles so it won't tangle.

8 Pull needle A upward so that the stitches slide onto the cable, keep both cable of A and point of B in your left hand.

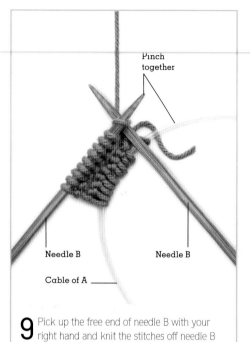

Pinch together

Needle B

Needle B

Cable of A

9 Pick up the free end of needle B with your right hand and knit the stitches off needle B in your left hand. Pinch the tip of needle B to the cable of needle A to prevent a gap at the join.

10 Complete the first side of tube 1. The needles now face each other as shown. Slide tube 1 down onto the cable, keeping the end of needle B in your right hand.

Needle B ——— Needle A

Needle B ——— Needle A

11 Slide tube 2 up to the tips of the other end of needle B, and holding this end in your left hand knit the first side of tube 2 with needle B.

12 Turn your work so that the working end of yarn is on the tip in your left hand, and slide a tube to each end. You will now see that you are halfway around both tubes.

13 Swap point protectors to needle B. Position needles as step 7, but reverse the needle positions so that B is on the left.

14 Work as step 8 but pull needle B upward.

15 Pick up the free end of needle A with your right hand and knit the stitches off the needle A tip in your left hand. Complete the second side of tube 2, then slide this down onto the cable. Needles facing as in step 10.

16 Slide tube 1 up to the tips at the other end of needle A and knit the second side of tube 1 with needle A. Repeat steps 7–16, swapping point protectors as shown.

Needle B

Needle B

HELIX KNITTING

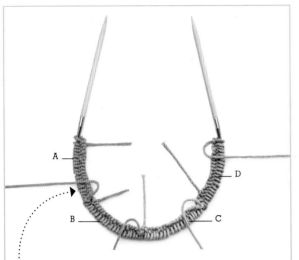

1 Cast on a quarter of the total number of stitches required in each color, (for example if 80 are stitches required, cast on 20 in A, 20 in B, 20 in C, and 20 in D). Leave yarns attached.

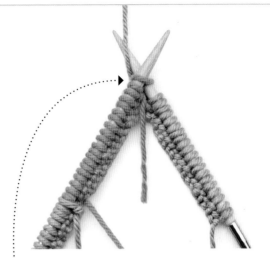

2 Without turning the needle, start to knit the color A stitches off the left needle using the working thread of D. At color joins, do not pull the new thread tight but keep the stitches even, otherwise the stripes will become distorted. Knit until all A stitches are worked.

3 Pick up the working thread of A and knit the next color. Continue to the end of each color, picking up yarn above next color.

4 After one round, there will be no yarn waiting at the end of the last color, so work to the point at which the next yarn is attached, pick it up and continue as step 3.

To work on double-pointed needles, using A, cast on, knit one round and join circle. Next round, knit a quarter of the stitches in A, followed by a quarter in the other three colors, one after the other on the next round. Continue as steps 2–4.

Circular knitting **127**

WORKING WITH A SET OF FOUR DOUBLE-POINTED NEEDLES

1 Your knitting instructions will specify how many double-pointed needles to use for the project you are making—either a set of four or a set of five. When working with a set of four double-pointed needles, first cast on all the stitches required onto a single needle. ....

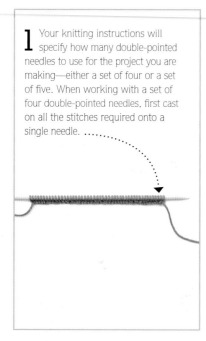

2 Slip some of the stitches off onto two other needles—your knitting pattern will tell you precisely how many to place on each needle. Ensure that the bottoms of the cast-on loops are all facing inward.

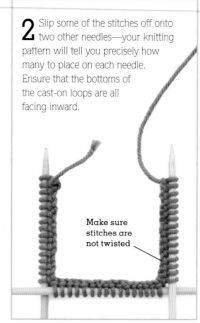

Make sure stitches are not twisted

3 Place a stitch marker between the first and second stitches on the first needle to mark the beginning of the round. Then pull the first and third needles close together and start to knit with the fourth needle. Knit around and around in this way as for knitting with a circular needle.

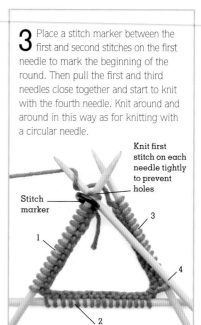

Knit first stitch on each needle tightly to prevent holes

Stitch marker

1

3

4

2

WORKING WITH A SET OF FIVE DOUBLE-POINTED NEEDLES

1 Cast on, distribute the stitches and position a stitch marker as for working with four needles, but distribute the stitches over four needles.

Stitch marker

Make sure stitches are not twisted

1   4

2   3

2 Use the fifth needle to knit. Knit the first stitch tightly to close the gap between the first cast-on stitch and the last.

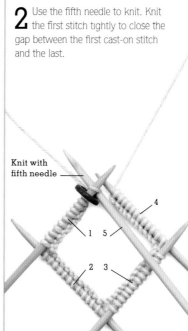

Knit with fifth needle

4

1   5

2   3

3 When all stitches on the first needle have been knitted onto the spare needle, use this empty needle to work the stitches on the second needle. Continue around and around like this, slipping the stitch marker from the left needle to the right needle when it is reached.

SPIRAL KNITTING

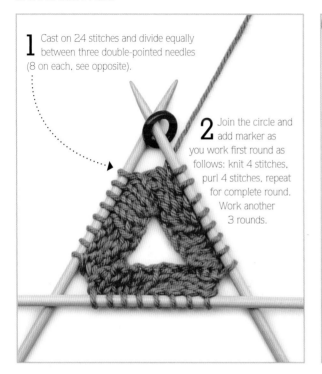

1 Cast on 24 stitches and divide equally between three double-pointed needles (8 on each, see opposite).

2 Join the circle and add marker as you work first round as follows: knit 4 stitches, purl 4 stitches, repeat for complete round. Work another 3 rounds.

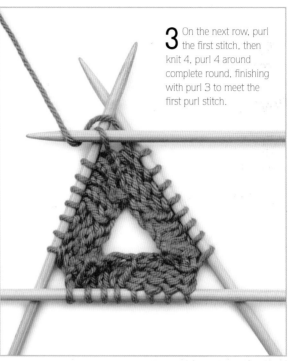

3 On the next row, purl the first stitch, then knit 4, purl 4 around complete round, finishing with purl 3 to meet the first purl stitch.

4 This has moved the whole rib one stitch over. Continue moving the rib one stitch in the same direction every four rows as you work the required length.

5 This technique is particularly successful as jewelry when it incorporates fancy and sparkly yarns or beading.

Reverse, twice knit, and Tunisian

Reverse knitting is simply a quicker way of working. The techniques produce a quite different, firmer, and less stretchy result than traditional knitting. In some cases the results can look more like crochet than knitting and can be used for a similar effect.

Reverse knitting

Reverse, or backward, knitting is useful for narrow areas when frequent turning is otherwise required. When working reverse knit stitches on stockinette stitch, every row is worked from the right side. Reverse knitting purl stitches is more unusual.

REVERSE KNIT STITCH

1 At the end of a knit row, do not turn the work.

2 Insert the left needle into the back of the first stitch on the right needle. Bring yarn forward between the needles from left to right.

3 Slide the right needle along the left needle and slip the loop over the left tip, then slide the right needle down out of the old stitch.

REVERSE PURL STITCH

1 At the end of a purl row, do not turn the work. Keep yarn at front.

2 Insert the left needle from back to front through the left leg of the first stitch on the right needle and in front of the right needle. Take the yarn in a counterclockwise circle and between the needles from right to left.

3 Slide the left needle through the stitch backward under the right needle to catch the loop. Slide the left needle to the right to slip the old stitch over the right tip.

Twice knit knitting

Twice knit is not stretchy, which makes it very dense, and it should be worked on larger needles than normal for the yarn. The stitches will work out wider than the rows unless larger needles are used, and work will be very slow to grow.

1 Cast on with twice knitted cast-on (see p. 47).

2 Knit two stitches together. Drop only the first stitch, leaving the second on the left needle.

3 Insert the right needle into both the remaining stitch and the following one on the left needle and knit them together. Repeat this step to end of row.

4 Every row is knitted the same way. The resulting fabric is firm, slow to unravel or snag, and can be cut much like a woven fabric.

Tunisian knitting

Tunisian knitting results in flat, dense, and thick fabric that looks a little like crochet. It can be worked on standard needles, although it is usually worked loosely or on slightly larger needles than normal for the yarn. The first row is always a wrong side row.

1 Slip one stitch knitwise, then make a yarn-over from front to back, taking yarn right around needle and to the front. Slip the next stitch knitwise, yarn over. Repeat this slip and yarn-over along the row.

Slip stitch

2 The last yarn-over will be loose, so hold it at the front with your left thumb. Turn the work, keeping thumb and yarn-over in place (it will now be at the back of the work).

3 Work the next row by knitting each yarn-over and stitch together through back of loop (k2 tbl). To start the row, insert the right needle into the back of the first stitch and yarn-over on left needle, bring yarn-over thread around the right needle (see p. 75) and knit yarn-over and first stitch together. Repeat steps 1–3.

4 It is easier to work this k2 tbl by inserting the right needle tip into the front of the stitch and yarn-over, and then sliding it backward over the left needle shaft before knitting into the back of both.

5 Cast off with a US9 (UK5/5.5mm) needle or larger, by knitting three stitches, and passing the first over the second two. Knit another stitch and repeat the pass over. Repeat along edge.

Finishing details

Finishing, as its name suggests, is the final stage of a project. Details that will make your knitting easier to assemble and look more professional, such as adding borders, hems, pockets, and fastenings, can, with a little planning, be incorporated into the actual knitting itself.

Picking up stitches

Picking up edges is a technique that even experienced knitters can find challenging. Careful preparation and lots of practice will help. Try it out on small pieces of knitting to perfect the technique before moving on to more important projects.

CAST-ON/OFF EDGE

With RS facing, insert the needle in the first stitch. Leaving a long, loose end, wrap the yarn around the tip and pull it through, as if knitting a stitch. Continue, picking up and knitting one stitch through every cast-on or cast-off stitch.

ALONG ROW-ENDS

1 On lightweight or medium-weight yarn, pick up about three stitches for every four row-ends. To begin, mark out the row-ends on the right side of the knitting, placing a pin on the first of every four row-ends as shown here.

2 Pick up and knit the stitches as for picking up stitches along a cast-on edge, inserting the tip through the center of the edge stitches. Skip every fourth row-end.

Remove pin before picking up stitch

Skipped row-ends

WITH A CROCHET HOOK

1 Use a hook that fits through the stitches. With RS facing, insert the hook through the first stitch, wrap the hook behind and around the yarn from left to right and pull through.

Yarn going to ball

Yarn tail

2 Transfer the loop on the hook onto a needle. Pull yarn to tighten. Repeat, transferring the loops to the needle.

TIPS FOR PICKING UP STITCHES

• **A yarn in a contrasting color** is used in the step-by-step instructions for picking up stitches to clearly illustrate the process. You can hide picking-up imperfections, however, if you use a matching yarn. For a contrasting border, switch to the new color on the first row of the border.

• **Always pick up** and knit stitches with the right side of the knitting facing you, since picking up stitches creates a ridge on the wrong side.

• **Your knitting pattern** will specify which needle size to use for picking up stitches—usually one size smaller than the size used for the main knitting.

• **After you have picked up** the required number of stitches, work the border following the directions in your pattern, whether it is ribbing, seed stitch, garter stitch, or a fold-over hem.

• **It is difficult to pick up stitches** "evenly" along an edge. To help, try casting it off again, either looser or tighter. If this doesn't work, pull out the border and try again, adjusting the number of stitches or spreading them out in a different way. Alternatively, try a smaller needle size if the border looks too stretched, or a larger needle size if it looks too tight.

ALONG A CURVED EDGE

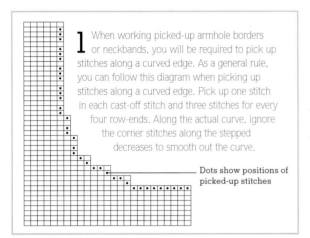

1 When working picked-up armhole borders or neckbands, you will be required to pick up stitches along a curved edge. As a general rule, you can follow this diagram when picking up stitches along a curved edge. Pick up one stitch in each cast-off stitch and three stitches for every four row-ends. Along the actual curve, ignore the corner stitches along the stepped decreases to smooth out the curve.

Dots show positions of picked-up stitches

2 Once all the stitches have been picked up, work the border as instructed in your knitting pattern.

A picked-up border with five rows of single ribbing

Selvages

The selvage can make all the difference to a free edge and there are many methods that are decorative as well as functional. Loose edges can be tightened with chain or slipped garter and rolling edges controlled with a garter selvage. Both selvages do not have to be worked the same.

GARTER SELVAGE

1 This is best for edges that will not be sewn together, since it can make a bumpy seam. It helps the edge of stockinette stitch to lie flat. Each "bump" equals two rows.

2 On stockinette stitch, knit the first and last stitch of every row.

SLIPPED GARTER SELVAGE

Firmer than garter selvage.

1 Slip first stitch knitwise and knit last stitch on all rows.

2 The resulting edge is firmer than garter selvage (see p. 133), and smoother. The slipped stitches can aid picking up on some projects.

DOUBLE SLIPPED GARTER SELVAGE

Good for slightly decorative free edges.

1 Work all rows the same. Insert the right needle into back of first stitch from right to left and slip the stitch.

2 Knit the second stitch. Work as pattern to two from end of row and knit the last two stitches.

CHAIN SELVAGE

Best for picking up stitches into (see pp. 132–133), crochet edgings, and backstitch (but not mattress stitch) seams (see p. 149).

1 On stockinette stitch, on all right side rows slip first stitch knitwise, and knit last stitch. On all wrong side rows, slip first stitch purlwise, and purl last stitch. ....

2 On garter stitch, with yarn in front slip first stitch purlwise, yarn back and knit to end. ....

PICOT LOOP SELVAGE

1 Right side rows, insert right needle knitwise into first two stitches, bring yarn around front of right needle from left to right and work a yarn-over (see p. 75) while knitting first two stitches together. Knit to last two stitches, slip them knitwise one by one and insert left needle into front to make an ssk decrease (see p. 78).

2 Wrong side rows, loosely work a purl yarn-over (see p. 74, hold it open with your thumb, if necessary), and purl rest of row. On garter stitch, purl first and last two stitches.

PICOT SELVAGE

1 On stockinette stitch on a knit row, knit-on cast-on two stitches, then cast off knitwise the same two stitches.

2 Slip the remaining stitch on the left needle without twisting onto the right needle. Knit to end of row.

3 On the purl row, cast on two stitches as step 1, yarn to front and cast off both stitches purlwise (see p. 51).

4 Yarn to front, slip remaining stitch on left needle, without twisting, onto right needle. Purl to end of row.

FRINGED SELVAGE

1 For a four-stitch fringed selvage, using backward loop cast-on (see p. 35), cast on knit width plus an extra eight stitches. Work as many rows as required in stockinette stitch or a variation of knit and purl stitches. On the last row drop four stitches at each end of the row. Cast off the remaining stitches.

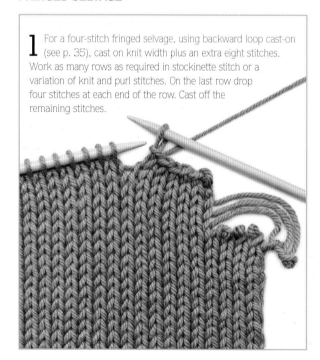

2 Unravel the edge stitches all the way down the fabric. To make the fringe straight, thread a long needle through all loops and block them while stretched flat (see p. 149).

Blocking will help straighten the fringe

Buttonholes

The simplest form of buttonhole is an eyelet, but there are techniques for larger, stronger ones that will take different sized buttons. Although horizontal buttonholes are the most common, vertical and diagonal variations are also included in this section.

POSITIONING BUTTONS AND BUTTONHOLES

Decide on the number of buttons before knitting buttonholes. Work holes to match button size. Top and bottom buttons are usually positioned between ½in (1cm) and 1¼in (3cm) from neck and hem edge. Start buttonholes at least 3 stitches from the edge. Count rows and stitches, since measuring may be inaccurate. For vertically worked bands, knit and attach the buttonband first. Mark the top and bottom button position with thread.

40	½in (1cm) 5 rows
40	
40	19¾in (50cm) 240 rows
40	
40	½in (1cm) 5 rows
40	

1 Knit the buttonhole band, working the calculated number of rows between buttonholes, allowing two rows for a two-row buttonhole. Work vertical buttonhole rows so that they center on the marker.

2 For a horizontally worked picked up buttonband, count stitches rather than rows to calculate the spacing, as described in step 1.

MAKING BUTTON LOOPS

1 Leaving a short loose end, pass the needle from back to front through the knitting at one end of the loop position and through the knitting again at the other end of the loop.

Mark width of loop with pins   Use a blunt-ended yarn needle

2 Pass the needle again through the knitting from back to front at the first pin. This creates a doubled strand for the base of the loop.

Short yarn end

3 Work buttonhole stitches tightly over the doubled strand and the short yarn end. Secure the yarn to the knitting. Pass the yarn through a few buttonhole stitches and trim.

KNITTED BUTTON LOOP

1 Using cable cast-on (see p. 37), cast on as many stitches as required for length of loop. Next row, cast off all stitches. ....

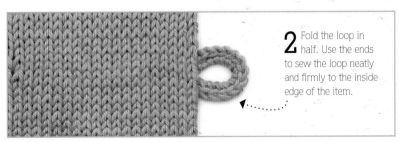

2 Fold the loop in half. Use the ends to sew the loop neatly and firmly to the inside edge of the item.

CHAIN EYELET

1 For a chain eyelet on a stockinette-stitch ground, begin by creating a yarn-over on the right needle (see p. 74). Knit the next two stitches together (see p. 77).

Yarn-over

2 The yarn-over creates a hole in the knitting and the k2tog decrease compensates for the extra loop so that the knitting remains the same width.

3 On the following row, purl the yarn-over in the usual way. A single chain eyelet is shown here so that its structure is clear, but eyelets can be arranged separated by several rows and several stitches or sitting side by side.

OPEN EYELET

1 For an open eyelet on a stockinette stitch ground, work a yarn-over on the right needle (see p. 74). Then work a "s1 k1 psso" decrease (see p. 78) after the yarn-over.

Yarn-over

2 The yarn-over creates a hole and the decrease compensates for the extra loop so that the knitting remains the same width.

3 On the following row, purl the yarn-over in the usual way. Open eyelets can be arranged in various ways to create any number of different textures.

An open eyelet can be used as a buttonhole

REINFORCED EYELET BUTTONHOLE

1 On a knit row, work to position of buttonhole. Make a yarn-over (see p. 74). Work to end of row. ·········

2 On next row, slip the yarn-over purlwise and make another front to back yarn-over. Work to end of row.

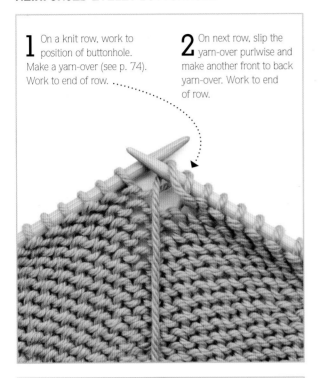

3 On next row, slip the stitch before the yarn-overs knitwise. Knit both yarn-overs together but do not drop from left needle. ·········

4 Pass slipped stitch over the newly made stitch. Knit three stitches together (the yarn-overs and the following stitch). Work to end of row. ·········

5 This buttonhole is stronger and neater than a simple eyelet buttonhole (see opposite).

ONE ROW HORIZONTAL BUTTONHOLE

A strong buttonhole that is worked on stockinette stitch in this example, but looks particularly neat on a garter stitch or reverse stockinette stitch project.

1 Work to buttonhole position (a knit row on reverse stockinette stitch). Yarn to front. Slip one stitch purlwise. Yarn back.

2 Slip one stitch purlwise and pass previous stitch over. Repeat this step across the number of buttonhole stitches required.

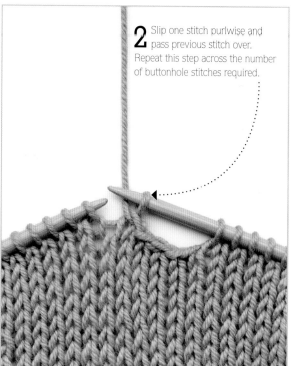

3 Slip last stitch on right needle back to the left. Turn work. Yarn back.

4 Cast on the number of stitches for the buttonhole using cable cast-on (see p. 37). Cast on one more stitch, bring yarn forward after making stitch but before placing it on left needle. Turn work.

5 Slip one stitch knitwise and pass the last cast-on stitch over it. Work rest of row.

CAST-OFF HORIZONTAL BUTTONHOLE

1 On a knit row, work to buttonhole position. Work two more stitches before passing one over the other in a knitwise cast-off (see p. 50) for the required number of buttonhole stitches. When the last cast-off loop is on right needle, slip the first stitch on left needle onto right needle and pass last cast-off loop over this stitch. Pull yarn tight. Work next row to buttonhole.

2 For simple completion, turn work and use cable cast-on (see p. 37). When last cast-on loop is still on right needle bring yarn to front between needles and transfer the stitch to the left needle. Yarn to back, turn, and knit rest of row. Buttonhole is now completed.

3 For advanced completion using buttonhole cast-on, skip step 2, only working steps 3–5. Drop left needle (use point protector to retain stitches if necessary) and work only with right. Hold yarn and needle in right hand. With left thumb pointing downward, pick up yarn from behind, and wind thumb to right in an counterclockwise circle so yarn crosses near needle. Insert right needle into front thumb loop.

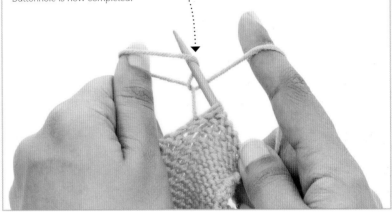

4 Bring left index finger from beneath, catching the yarn. Take yarn left behind needle and then wind to right, over needle.

5 Slip thumb loop over point of right needle. Hold new loop in place with right index finger and tighten yarn with left hand, making sure the loop goes all round the needle. Repeat for each cast-on stitch. Knit to end of row.

VERTICAL BUTTONHOLE

1 This example is in stockinette stitch. Work to position of buttonhole. Slip the stitches that will be to the left of the buttonhole onto a stitch holder. Turn work.

2 Work right side of buttonhole starting with a purl row, making a chain selvage (see p. 135) by slipping first edge stitch purlwise on all wrong side rows, and knitting last edge stitch on all right side rows.

3 Once right side is long enough, finish on a purl side row, cut yarn with a long tail and slip right side stitches onto another holder. Slip held stitches back onto left needle with knit side facing. Join in new end of yarn (leaving a long tail) and make a right lifted increase (see p. 72) between the first and second stitches.

4 Slip the last stitch knitwise on the next and all wrong side rows and knit it into the back of the first stitch on all right side rows. This creates a variation of a chain selvage on the left side of the buttonhole.

5 When both sides have equal rows, making sure you finish on a purl row, cut the yarn with a long tail and restore all stitches to the needles in the correct order. Join yarn in and work a complete row, working the two selvage stitches of the buttonhole together. Sew in ends neatly.

DIAGONAL BUTTONHOLE

1 Working in stockinette stitch, knit to position of buttonhole. Slip the stitches that will be to the left of the buttonhole onto a stitch holder. Turn work. Slip first stitch purlwise. Make a yarn-over. Purl to end.

2 Knit next row to yarn-over, and knit into back of yarn-over, twisting it to close the hole. Knit last stitch. Repeat for required length of buttonhole, ending with a purl row. Repeat knit instruction in step 1.

3 Cut yarn with a long tail and slip right side stitches onto another holder. Slip held stitches back onto the left needle with knit side facing. Join in new end of yarn and make a right leaning increase (see p. 72) between the first and second stitches.

4 Knit into the back of the first stitch and knit to end. Purl next row to three stitches from end. Purl next two stitches together and slip last stitch knitwise. Repeat this step for required length of buttonhole, ending with a purl row.

5 Cut yarn with a long tail and restore all stitches to needles in the correct order. Join yarn in and work a complete row, working the two selvage stitches of the buttonhole together. Sew in ends neatly. To slant the buttonhole the other way, reverse the increase and decrease.

Pockets

Patch pockets can be knitted separately and sewn on or picked up from the main knitting. Inset versions are particularly neat on garments and can be edged with textural and color stitch details, and even knitted in lighter yarns to avoid bulk

PICKED-UP PATCH POCKET

1 Work garment piece first. Baste the side and bottom position of the pocket on the garment with thin contrast-color yarn. To ensure a straight pocket bottom, either pick up into the row after welt or baste through left side of stitches along the base row.

2 Thread pocket yarn on a large-eyed needle, take the end to the wrong side and secure it, leaving a long tail. Have a knitting needle ready to receive stitches as they are made. Starting at the lower right-hand corner of the marked stitches, insert a crochet hook through the middle of the "V" of the first stitch, under the top loop and back out to the front. Lay the yarn from right to left into the hook, and draw a loop of yarn through.

3 Slip loop onto right needle. Repeat steps 2 and 3 to left along the row for each pocket base stitch.

4 Beginning with a wrong side row, work as many rows as necessary for the pocket depth, adding a ribbed or patterned welt as desired. Cast off.

5 Sew sides in place with mattress stitch (see p. 149) using the yarn ends if possible. Remove basting stitches.

HORIZONTAL INSET POCKET

1 Knit the pocket lining before you knit the garment piece, this will be two stitches wider than the cast off for the pocket. Leave on needle after working last knit row or put on stitch holder.

2 With right side facing, work to pocket position. Cast-off knitwise (see p. 50) the stitches for the pocket opening and knit to end of row.

3 Turn and purl back to one stitch from pocket position. Take needle with lining stitches on it in left hand, and purl last main stitch and first lining stitch together.

4 Purl across lining stitches. Purl last stitch together with first one on left needle. Continue. Complete garment piece.

5 An alternative to step 2 is to place the opening stitches without casting off onto a stitch holder. This allows you to knit an edging to the pocket later on.

6 When sewing garment together, whipstitch the lining to the garment without pulling the stitches too tight. This example has a contrast lining, but the lining would normally be made in the main yarn.

1 The opening is at the left of the actual pocket in this example, and the lining is worked at the same time as the pocket front. On a right side row, work to pocket position, slip remaining stitches on left needle onto a stitch holder.

2 Work front of pocket: Turn work and work garter stitch edge border by knitting first two stitches, purling the rest of the row. On next row, work to two from end and then knit both edge stitches. Continue to work rows, with border stitches included, for depth of pocket. Finish pocket front by working a purl row and slip stitches onto a stitch holder. Cut yarn with a long end.

3 The right side and lining is worked in one: With right side facing, slip stitches off first stitch holder onto a needle, unless you use a double-pointed needle, you may need to transfer them from this needle to one that has its tip facing to the right. Join in yarn.

4 Cable cast-on (see p. 37) the number of stitches required for width of pocket lining. Turn and work the same number of rows for the lining and left side as were worked for the pocket front. End with a purl row.

5 Join top of pocket. With right side facing, slip stitches off second stitch holder onto a needle pointing right (stitch holder should be pointing left). Knit next row. At pocket position, place lining needle behind left needle and knit them together. Complete row.

6 Complete piece and sew lining to garment front.

Hems

A traditional ribbed hem is often knitted at the start of a garment, whereas others may be sewn on afterward. Color detail and stitch structures, such as garter stitch, seed stitch, or cables can be incorporated to add flair to hems. Hems make great cuffs and can be added vertically along front openings. They also make good accessory trims.

PICKED-UP HEM

1 Cast on length of hem using backward loop cast-on (see p. 35) with smaller needles. This example uses two colors to differentiate inner from outer, but this can also be a design feature. In contrast color, work required depth of inner hem in stockinette stitch, finishing on a knit row.

2 Change to main color and work another knit row as the fold row. On larger needles in main color, recommence stockinette stitch with a knit row, and work until inner and outer are the same length, finishing with a purl row.

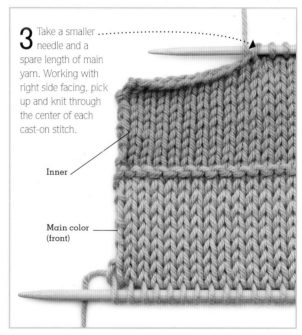

3 Take a smaller needle and a spare length of main yarn. Working with right side facing, pick up and knit through the center of each cast-on stitch.

Inner

Main color (front)

4 These stitches may have to be transferred to another needle, as the needle must point in the same direction as that of the hem stitches. Fold the hem up along the fold line with right side out. Hold the two needles together in the left hand.

5 Taking a larger needle and rejoining main yarn if necessary, knit the corresponding stitches of both needles together onto the right needle.

6 Block hem with garment to achieve the final effect. (see p.149)

PICOT HEM

1 Using smaller needles, cast on an even number of stitches to the length of the hem using single cast-on (see p. 35).

2 Work required depth of hem in stockinette stitch, ending with a purl row.

3 Next row, knit first two stitches together (see p. 77), make a yarn-over by bringing yarn forward and back over the needle (see p. 75). Repeat to end of row.

4 Change to larger needles. Knit stitches and yarn-overs on first row, and work to equal depth of hem in stockinette stitch, ending on a purl row.

Yarn-over lace holes

5 When piece is completed, fold the hem up at lace holes with wrong sides together. Pin so that the stitches are in line. Working from the wrong side, whipstitch in place along a row using hem yarn and blunt-ended needle as follows: Insert needle into a reverse stitch loop and then its vertically matching cast-on loop, pull yarn through and repeat. Do not allow the sewing to pucker the knitting.

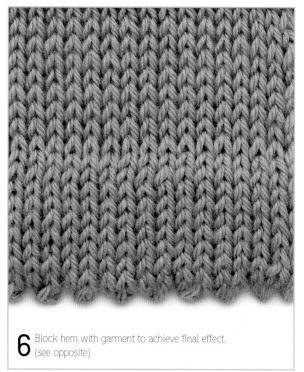

6 Block hem with garment to achieve final effect. (see opposite)

Blocking

Always refer to your yarn label before blocking. Textured stitch patterns, such as garter stitch, ribbing, and cables, are best wet blocked or steamed extremely gently so that their texture is not altered—they should not be pressed or stretched.

WET BLOCKING

If your yarn allows, wet blocking is the best way to even out your knitting. Using lukewarm water, either wash the piece or simply wet it. Squeeze and lay it flat on a towel, then roll the towel to squeeze out more moisture. Pin the piece into shape on layers of dry towels covered with a sheet. Leave to dry completely.

STEAM BLOCKING

Only steam block if your yarn allows. Pin the piece to the correct shape, then place a clean damp cloth on top. Use a warm iron to create steam, barely touching the cloth. Do not rest the iron on the knitting, and avoid any garter stitch or ribbed areas. Before removing the pins, let the piece dry completely.

Seams

The most popular seam techniques for knitting are mattress stitch, edge-to-edge stitch, backstitch, and whipstitch. Cast-off and grafted seams are sometimes called for and learning to graft open stitches together for a seamless join is very useful.

TIPS

• **Block knitted pieces** before sewing together. After seams are completed, open them out and steam very lightly if the yarn allows.
• **Always use** a blunt-ended yarn needle for all seams on knitting. A pointed needle will puncture the yarn strands and you won't be able to pull the yarn through the knitting successfully.
• **Although the seams** are shown here worked in a contrasting yarn for clarity, use a matching yarn for all seams.
• **If knitting** is in a fancy yarn, find a smooth strong yarn of a similar

color to sew in. It is generally better, particularly with mattress stitch, to work with shorter lengths as long strands become weakened and may break.
• **Before starting a seam,** pin the knitting together at wide intervals. At the start of the seam, secure the yarn to the edge of one piece of knitting with two or three overcast stitches.
• **Make seams firm** but not too tight. They should have a little elasticity, to match the elasticity of the knitted fabric.

MATTRESS STITCH

1 Mattress stitch is practically invisible and is the best seam technique for ribbing and stockinette stitch. Start by aligning the edges of the pieces to be seamed with both the right sides facing you.

2 Insert the needle from the front through center of first knit stitch on one piece of knitting and up through center of stitch two rows above. Repeat on the other piece, working up the seam and pulling edges together.

FIGURE-EIGHT START FOR SEAMS

2 Bring needle from back to front through bottom stitch of right piece, as close to both edges as possible.

1 Lay pieces to be joined side by side, right sides facing you. Thread needle with knitting yarn or substitute (see Tips for seams, p. 149).

3 Take needle under left piece, and insert it from back to front through bottom edge stitch.

4 Take needle to right piece and repeat step 2. This makes a figure eight, which is a strong, neat start to a seam.

5 To use before mattress stitch, after step 4, take needle back under the left piece and bring it through the same place as before. This positions the first stitch in the correct place.

EDGE-TO-EDGE SEAM

This seam is suitable for most stitch patterns. To start, align the pieces of knitting with the wrong sides facing you. Work each stitch of the seam through the little bumps formed along the edges of knitting as shown.

Wrong sides

BACKSTITCH SEAM

Backstitch can be used for almost any seam on knitting, but is not suitable for super-bulky yarns.

1 Align the pieces of knitting with the right sides together. Make one stitch forward, and one stitch back into the starting point of the previous stitch as shown. Work the stitches as close to the edge of the knitting as possible.

Right sides of knitting together

WHIPPED STITCH SEAM

Other names for this seam are an oversewn seam or an overcast seam.

1 With the right sides together, insert the needle from back to front through both layers, working through the centers of the edge stitches (not through the bumps). Make each stitch in the same way.

Right sides of knitting together

GRAFTED SEAM

The seam can be worked along two pieces of knitting that have not been cast off or along two cast-off edges as shown here; the principle for both is the same.

1 With the right sides facing you, follow the path of a row of knitting along the seam as shown.

2 When worked in a matching yarn as here, the seam blends in completely and makes it look like a continuous piece of knitting.

GRAFTING OPEN STITCHES TOGETHER

"Waste" rows

Pieces to be joined must have the same number of stitches. Knit row stitches can be recognized as "V"s.

1 At the end of main knitting, do not cast off, but knit four rows of stockinette stitch "waste" rows in a thinner, contrast colored yarn. Leave on needles or holder.

2 When ready to join pieces, remove needle or holder. Lay pieces right side up, open edges facing as shown. Thread a blunt-ended needle, ideally with a long end from one of the rows to be grafted.

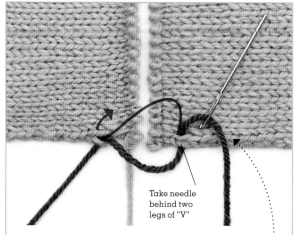

Take needle behind two legs of "V"

3 Insert needle from the back through the first main color stitch on the left piece (so it comes out through the "V" of the stitch).

4 Insert needle from front through main color edge loop on the right, across behind two "legs" (behind "V"), and out to the front between two stitches (between "V"s).

5 Continue, taking the needle back into the "V" of the left-hand stitch that it emerges from, behind the two "legs" and out of the next "V." Gently pull yarn until sewn stitch is same size as knit stitches. As you pull, fold the waste fabric under to close the gap.

6 Repeat, taking needle to right side.

7 Repeat steps 5 and 6 along the row. Secure the ends and unravel the waste yarns. With more experience it becomes possible to graft the pieces together right off the needles without knitting waste rows.

SEWING ON AN EDGING

Wrong side of edging

1 Pin the edging to the knitting with the right sides facing each other.

Right side of knitting

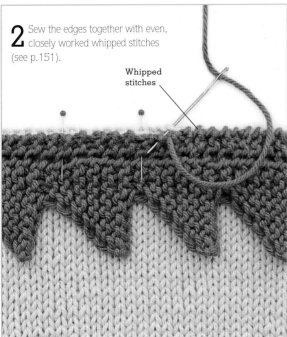

2 Sew the edges together with even, closely worked whipped stitches (see p.151).

Whipped stitches

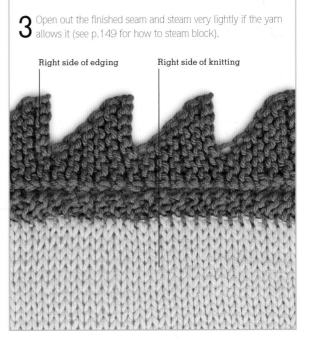

3 Open out the finished seam and steam very lightly if the yarn allows it (see p.149 for how to steam block).

Right side of edging   Right side of knitting

Cutting into your knitting

Cutting can be a time-saving way of completing projects, particularly for circular knitted garments. Hairy wool that clings to itself and felts slightly when washed is ideal. "Steek" or "bridge" are common terms for the extra stitches knitted where openings will later be cut. You can machine sew edges prior to picking up.

STEEKS OR BRIDGES

1 To work a steek as, for example, a cardigan opening, cast on an extra nine stitches for the steek at the center front. Work these stitches in one stitch vertical stripes if knitting Fair Isle and in stockinette stitch when working with one color. Use markers to identify the steek.

2 Work complete front. Block the piece and cut straight up the center stitch of the steek. If the knitting unravels easily, run a line of small machine stitches along inside the open edge to prevent them from unraveling further.

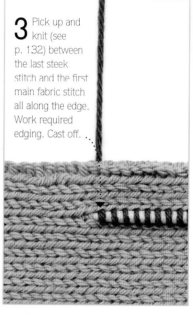

3 Pick up and knit (see p. 132) between the last steek stitch and the first main fabric stitch all along the edge. Work required edging. Cast off.

4 Turn work inside out, trim any unraveled ends with sharp scissors and whipstitch the cut edge down to the back of the main fabric using main color yarn. Sew back, crossing the first stitches.

5 The cut edge is neatly folded under and invisible on the right side of the completed cardigan opening.

Fastenings

Choose an appropriate size and material for your project. Although nylon and plastic fastenings are lighter and less obtrusive, metallic or contrast colored ones can make a statement. Riveted press snaps can be used; insert the shank between stitches and when connecting top to bottom, make sure there are no sharp edges to cut stitches.

ATTACHING PRESS SNAPS

Male side of the snap goes on the inside of the outer of a garment. Decide position of snaps. Measuring can be inaccurate; count exact stitches and rows on each piece and mark positions with contrast thread.

1 Make a knot and sew in end of thread at marker, catching only half of each strand of yarn so that stitches don't go through to right side. Place snap in position centrally over marker and insert needle inward through surface of yarn near a snap hole just below the snap edge, then bring it up through the snap hole.

2 Repeat this three or four times through each hole, never taking the needle through to the right side. Move needle to next hole and repeat. To secure thread, sew two small backstitches, then sew a loop, thread the needle back through and pull tightly to secure thread.

SEWING IN A ZIPPER

1 Match color and weight of zipper to yarn, and knit length of garment to match zipper lengths available. Work a garter stitch selvage (see p. 133) at the zipper edge.

2 Close the zipper. With RS facing, pin the top and bottom of knitting to the zipper first, making sure the teeth are covered by the knitted edge. Pin the center, then the centers of the remaining sections, easing the rows so they are evenly distributed. Pin horizontally rather than vertically. Do one side at a time and use plenty of pins.

3 Baste the zipper in place with contrast sewing thread, sewing between the same vertical lines of stitches.

4 With a sharp large-eyed needle and knitting yarn (or matching sewing thread), backstitch neatly upward from hem, sewing between the same vertical lines of stitches.

5 Turn garment inside out. With knitting yarn, or matching sewing thread, slip stitch outer edges of zipper to knitting, sewing into the back of the same vertical lines of stitches.

Embellishments

Plain knitting sometimes calls out for a little embellishment. Embroidery, a few well placed beads, or a decorative edging are good candidates for the perfect finishing touch. Pockets, collars, hems, and cuffs are ideal positions for these.

Bead knitting

Choose beads carefully; glass beads are attractive, but can weigh knitting down. Make sure that the bead hole is large enough for the yarn, or consider using a second thread or enclosing large beads. Beaded cast-on or cast-off make effective edgings.

THREADING BEADS ONTO YARN

Make sure you have the right beads before starting to thread them onto the yarn. Consider their size and weight. If your knitting is to be entirely covered with scattered beads, large heavy beads will be unsuitable as they would weigh the knitting down too much. Adding a little weight to the knitting can, however, produce the extra drape needed for a graceful shawl, scarf, or evening knit.

Thread the beads onto the yarn before you begin knitting. The last bead to be used is threaded on first and the first bead to be used is threaded on last. Fold a short length of sewing thread in half, thread both cut ends together through the eye of an ordinary sewing needle, and pass the end of the yarn through the sewing-thread loop. Thread the beads onto the sewing needle, over the thread and onto the yarn.

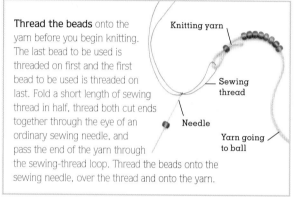

Knitting yarn
Sewing thread
Needle
Yarn going to ball

SLIP-STITCH BEADING

1 A chart is usually provided for positioning the beads on slip-stitch beading, unless only a few beads are to be added, in which case the bead placements will be within the written instructions. The sample chart here illustrates how slip-stitch beads are staggered. This is because the slipped stitches at the bead positions pull in the knitting and alternating the bead placements evens out the fabric.

□ = k on RS rows, p on WS rows   ● = place bead and slip stitch

8

1 (RS)

Rep = 4sts (x 8 rows)

2 The beads are placed on knit (right-side) rows. Knit to the position of the bead, then bring the yarn to the front (right side) of the work between the two needles. Slide the bead up close to the knitting and slip the next stitch purlwise from the left needle to right needle.

Slipping stitch purlwise

3 Take the yarn to the wrong side between the two needles, leaving the bead sitting on the right side in front of the stitch just slipped. Knit the next stitch firmly to tighten the strand holding the bead at the front.

Slipped stitch

SIMPLE GARTER-STITCH BEADING

1 This method can be used to create bands of beads along borders or at intervals for beaded stripes. Start with a right-side row and work at least three rows of plain garter stitch before adding any beads. On the next row (a wrong-side row), knit two edge stitches before adding a bead. Then push a bead up close to the knitting before working each stitch. At the end of the row, add the last bead when two stitches remain on the left needle, then knit the last two stitches.

Wrong side of knitting

2 Knit the next row with no beads. Alternate a bead row and a plain row to form a band of beads of the desired depth. This technique could be used to create a piece entirely covered with beads for a small bag, but would create a fabric too heavy for a large garment.

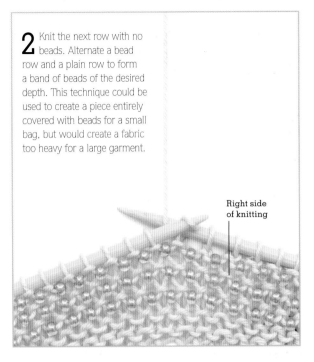

Right side of knitting

REVERSE-STITCH BEADING

1 Thread beads onto knitting yarn. Working in stockinette stitch, knit to one stitch before bead position. Yarn to front.

2 Purl one. The bead must sit tight against the right needle, so slide it along the yarn to this position and hold it there. Purl the next stitch. Yarn to back and work to next bead position.

Hold bead in position

INSET BEAD WITH A HOOK

1 Bead shows from both sides and is inset into the knitting. Knit to bead position.

2 Place bead on a fine crochet hook. Pick the next stitch off the left needle with the hook. Slide bead onto stitch and return it to left needle. Knit or purl the stitch as required. Needle and thread can be used instead of a crochet hook. In which case, make a loop of thread through stitch and slide bead down the thread.

Crochet hook

BEADED CAST-ON

1 Thread beads onto knitting yarn. Make a slip knot at the end of the yarn leaving a 4in (10cm) tail, and place on needle. Hold needle in right hand, yarn in left. Push a bead along the yarn between left hand and needle. Hold yarn and wrap it around thumb as shown, then insert right needle to work a backward loop cast-on (see p. 35). Make sure the bead remains under the needle.

2 Repeat for each cast-on stitch, or space the beads as required along the edge; this example has three stitches between each bead.

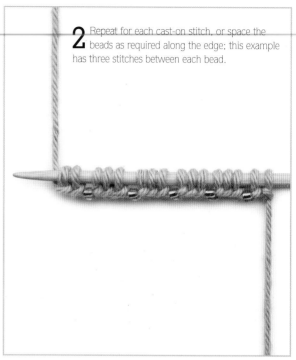

BEADED CAST-OFF

1 Cut a piece of main color yarn five times the width of the knitting. Thread one bead for each stitch to be beaded, less one, onto the yarn. Tie the last bead (which will not be worked) to the end of the yarn to prevent beads from sliding off.

2 With beaded yarn, knit first two stitches of cast-off. Pass second over first as normal. This leaves a selvage stitch for seaming.

3 Push a bead close to back of fabric. For a firm edge (as shown here), knit stitch drawing both bead and yarn through stitch. To alter lie of bead, change which side of the bead the stitch is passed over in step 4. For a dangling bead, knit the next stitch leaving bead at back as new loop is formed.

4 For either method, pass second stitch on right needle over first and off tip of needle.

5 Repeat steps 3 and 4 along the cast-off, either working one bead per stitch or some plain cast-offs in between, depending on size of bead and effect required.

6 The last stitch should not be beaded if it will be seamed, so remove and discard end bead, work last stitch plain and pull end through as normal.

TUBULAR POCKETS FOR LARGE BEADS

1 Knit to position of bead: Insert needle and knit front and back of the stitch (see p. 70), repeat on next stitch (or work across more stitches depending on bead size). Knit to next bead.

2 On next row, purl to bead position. Purl the first increased stitch wrapping yarn twice round needle, slip the second purlwise, knit the third wrapping yarn twice round needle, slip fourth purlwise. Purl to next bead.

3 On next row, at bead position: Knit the first stitch wrapping yarn twice round needle, yarn to front and slip the second purlwise releasing the wrapped loops, yarn to back, knit the third stitch wrapping yarn twice round needle, yarn to front, slip the fourth stitch purlwise releasing the wrapped loops as shown. Yarn to back and knit to next bead.

4 Repeat steps 2 and 3 once or twice more (depending on bead size).

5 Purl to bead position. Slip the first stitch onto the right needle, the second onto a cable needle, the third onto the right needle, and the fourth onto the cable needle. This opens the tubular pocket. Insert bead. Return the four stitches to the left needle in the correct order without twisting. Purl two together twice to close pocket. Purl to next bead.

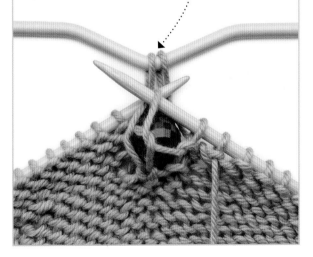

6 The completed pocket holds the bead in position. Large flat objects can be inserted in this way as well.

BEADED CLUSTERS AND LOOPS

1 Thread beads onto knitting yarn in desired color/shape sequence (here 4 small beads per cluster; 3 small, 1 larger, and 3 small per loop).

2 Cluster: work stockinette stitch to position of cluster. Yarn to front, slide 4 small beads along yarn. Yarn to back, tighten yarn and knit into back of next stitch and knit to next cluster position.

3 Loop: work in stockinette stitch to position of loop. Yarn to front, slide 3 small round beads, 1 larger one, and 3 more small ones along yarn to needles. Yarn to back. Knit into back of next stitch and knit to next loop. If the beads are heavy and a hole forms, try the following variation after taking yarn back: knit next stitch, but do not remove from left needle, knit into stitch again, sliding it off left needle afterward. Slip both loops of the stitch to the right needle, insert left needle into front of both loops and knit together (ssk).

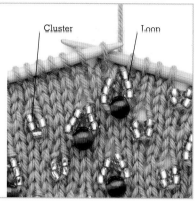

Cluster   Loop

Popcorns, bobbles, and curls

Popcorns and bobbles look similar but are worked differently. Bells are larger variations of tulip cluster bobbles but become partially detached from the knitting. Curls combine short rows with tubular knitting. Try using reverse knitting (see p. 130) to keep from turning the work.

POPCORNS

1 This example is worked on a knit row on stockinette stitch fabric. Knit to popcorn position.

2 Insert right needle as if to knit into next stitch, then knit into front, back, front, then back of the stitch. Slip stitch off needle. Four stitches are made from one. Knit to next popcorn position.

3 On next row, purl to popcorn position. Insert tip of left needle into second stitch on right needle and pass it over the first stitch and over the tip. Repeat with the third and fourth stitches.

4 Purl to next popcorn position. On next row, knit to next popcorn position and repeat steps 2–4 as required.

DETACHED BOBBLES

1 This example is worked on a knit row on stockinette stitch fabric, making a reverse-stockinette-stitch bobble. Knit to bobble position. Insert right needle knitwise into next stitch. Knit it without removing from left needle. Bring yarn to front between needles and purl into same stitch, yarn to back and knit it again, yarn to front, purl it again, yarn to back, knit it again.

2 Slide stitch off left needle. Five stitches are made from one.

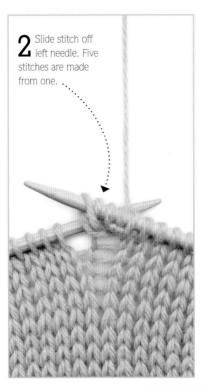

3 Turn the work. Knit across the five stitches and loops just made.

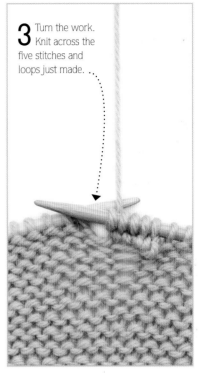

4 Turn and purl across the five stitches just worked. Yarn to back.

5 Insert tip of left needle into second stitch on right needle and pass it over the first stitch and over the tip of needle. Repeat with the third and fourth stitches. One bobble stitch left. Knit to next bobble position.

6 Repeat steps 1–5 to make next bobble. Bobbles can be purely decorative, or used as a functional fastener on garments or accessories.

TULIP CLUSTER BOBBLE

1 Makes a stockinette-stitch cluster on a reverse-stockinette-stitch fabric. On a right side row, purl to bobble position. Make five stitches out of one as in step 1 of bobbles (see p. 161). Purl to next bobble, or end of row.

2 Work three rows, working the background as stockinette stitch and the bobble as reverse stockinette stitch. (When background is knit, purl bobbles and vice versa).

Wrong side

3 Next row, with right side facing, purl to bobble position. Slip first bobble stitch to right needle, knit one and pass the slipped stitch over it. Knit one, k2tog, three stitches remain of bobble.

4 On next row, knit to bobble position and purl the three bobble stitches.

5 On next row, purl to bobble position, slip first stitch, k2tog and pass the first stitch over and off the right needle. Purl to next bobble.

6 Bobbles can be made larger by working more rows. For a more prominent version try working bells (opposite).

BELLS

1 This example works a stockinette-stitch bell on a reverse-stockinette-stitch background. With right side facing, purl to position of bell. Turn work and cable cast-on (see p. 37) 8 stitches onto what is temporarily the left needle. Turn work and work to next bell or end of row.

2 Work 5 more complete rows working background as reverse stockinette stitch and bell stitches as stockinette stitch.

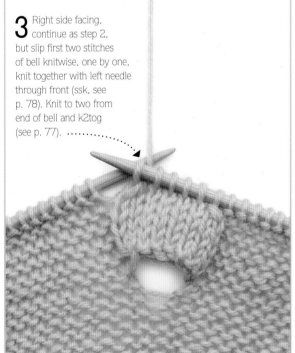

3 Right side facing, continue as step 2, but slip first two stitches of bell knitwise, one by one, knit together with left needle through front (ssk, see p. 78). Knit to two from end of bell and k2tog (see p. 77).

4 Repeat step 3 on every right side row, until only two stitches are left of bell. Knit these together on next knit row, and then knit last remaining stitch of bell together with the following one to complete the bell.

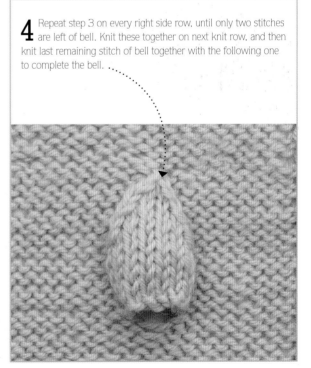

CURLS

1 Work in stockinette stitch. With wrong side facing, purl to position of curl in color A.

2 Work a purl right leaning increase using color B by picking up and purling into right side of stitch below next stitch (this is picked up the same as a right lifted increase on a knit row, see p. 71).

3 Purl one stitch in color A. Repeat this increase, purl one sequence across the width of the curl (six for this example, so the curl will be twelve stitches wide). Purl to end of row. ......

4 Knit to curl in color A. Color A and B at back. Knit all the color B stitches in color B, taking yarn forward and back to slip each color A stitch purlwise in between. Turn at end of curl. ......

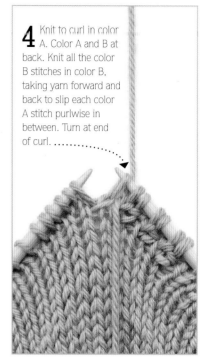

5 Keep color A at front. In color B, purl all color B stitches, taking yarn back and forward to slip each color A stitch in between. Turn at end of curl.

6 Repeat steps 4 and 5 two or more times, working only over curl stitches. ......

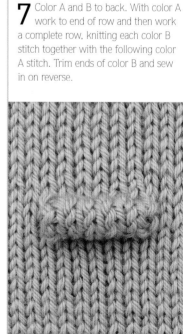

7 Color A and B to back. With color A work to end of row and then work a complete row, knitting each color B stitch together with the following color A stitch. Trim ends of color B and sew in on reverse.

Embroidery on knitting

Duplicate stitch, bullion stitch, lazy daisies, and chain stitch are most commonly used on knitting, although running and satin stitch can be very attractive. Use a smooth yarn that is the same weight as that used for the knitting, or slightly thicker, together with a blunt-ended needle to keep from splitting the knitting yarn.

DUPLICATE STITCH CHART

As duplicate stitch embroidery imitates and covers the knit stitches on the right side of the stockinette stitch, you can work any charted colorwork motif using the technique. (Cross stitch books are also good sources of motifs for duplicate stitch.) The completed embroidered motif will look as if it has been knitted into the fabric.

DUPLICATE STITCH WORKED HORIZONTALLY

1 Secure the embroidery yarn to the wrong side of the stockinette stitch, then pass the needle from back to front through the center of a knit stitch, and pull the yarn through. Next, insert the needle from right to left behind the knit stitch above as shown and pull the yarn through gently so it "mirrors" the knit stitch size. ....

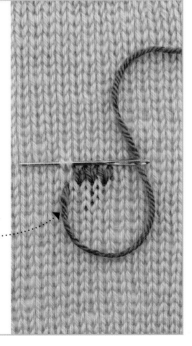

2 Insert the needle from right to left into the knit stitch below and out at the center of the next knit stitch to the left to complete the stitch as shown. Continue in this way, tracing the path of the knitting horizontally.

DUPLICATE STITCH WORKED VERTICALLY

1 Secure the embroidery yarn on the wrong side of the stockinette stitch, then pass the needle from back to front through the center of a knit stitch and pull the yarn through. Next, insert the needle from right to left behind the knit stitch above, as shown, and pull the yarn through.

2 Insert the needle from front to back and to front again under the top of the stitch below so it comes out in the center of the stitch just covered, as shown. Continue in this way, tracing the path of the knitting vertically.

SATIN STITCH

1 Secure yarn on the wrong side. Bring needle through to front between two stitches, at one side of the shape to be worked.

2 Take needle to back between two stitches at the opposite side of the shape.

3 Bring the needle to the front again at the original side, but spacing it a yarn-width away by angling the needle very slightly while at back of work. The stitches should lie flat and parallel to each other.

4 Continue to work the shape in long smooth stitches that do not pucker the fabric.

RUNNING STITCH

1 Secure yarn on wrong side of work. Bring needle through to front between two stitches, at the end of the line to be worked.

2 Take needle to back between two stitches a measured number of stitches or rows to the right (or left).

3 Repeat, spacing the stitches in an even pattern as required being careful not to pucker the fabric.

BULLION STITCH

To begin the stitch, secure the yarn on the wrong side and bring the needle through to the right side at one end of the position for the stitch. Then, insert the needle through to the back a short distance from the starting point and out to the front again at the starting point. Wrap the yarn at least six times around the needle close to the knitting and holding the wraps with your fingers, pull the needle carefully through the wraps. To complete the stitch, reinsert the needle through the knitting at the same place (as shown by the arrow). Arrange the bullion stitches in spirals to form rose shapes, or as here to form simple star or flower-petal shapes.

LAZY DAISY STITCH

Lazy daisy stitches are individual chain stitches held down at the loop end by a short stitch. They are traditionally used to form flower shapes. To begin the stitch, secure the yarn on the wrong side and bring the needle through at the center of the flower. Reinsert the needle through to the back at the starting point and bring it out to the front a short distance away as shown. Secure the loop with a short stitch. Work all the "petals" in the same way, starting each one at the flower center.

CHAIN STITCH ON STRIPES

Knitted stripes can be turned into a plaid or check pattern with simple vertical lines of chain stitch. Bring a blunt-ended yarn needle out in position for the first stitch. Reinsert the needle where it emerged and bring the tip out a short distance below with the yarn looped under it. Pull the yarn through. To continue, insert the needle back into the hole from which it has just emerged and bring it out a short distance below.

EMBROIDERED SMOCKING

Smocking draws the knitting in, so knit the fabric one and half times the required width.

1 Cast on a multiple of 8 plus 3 extra stitches (35 in this example). Work a wide rib fabric starting with 3 purl stitches and 1 knit stitch that repeats across the row, ending with 3 purl stitches. This is the right side. Work 30 rows and cast off.

2 Mark second rib stitch from right four rows up work from cast on. Thread a needle with contrast yarn, secure yarn to right side back of work and bring needle from back to front just between last purl stitch and the knit stitch of the marked rib stitch.

3 Working to left, reinsert needle to the back after the third rib knit stitch. Rethread yarn in same direction once more, making sure not to catch the yarn with the needle and ending with the needle at the back. Gently pull the yarn to gather the two ribs together. Continue along the row, working into each pair of rib stitches as shown. Gather each wound stitch as it is completed. Fasten and cut yarn at the other end.

4 Move four rows up and work next gathers. Refasten yarn to right edge, bring needle from back to front just before first rib knit stitch, reinsert just after second rib knit stitch, thread yarn around and gather as in step 3. Repeat along row, starting by bringing the yarn to front after the next three purl stitches as described in step 3. Continue alternating the stitches as step 3 and 4, spacing each repeat four rows apart up the fabric.

3-D embellishments

Surface embellishments and edge decorations can be attached to knitting once it is completed. These are easy and fun to make and extremely effective, but remember to buy extra yarn. Simple tools are required to make tassels, while a specially worked cast-on, cast-off, or selvage will make adding a fringe easier.

TASSELS

Piece of board cut to size

1 Select a template approximately the length of the finished tassel; this can be cut cardboard, but a book is often ideal. Holding the end with your thumb, wrap the yarn repeatedly around the template using single or varied colors. Fifty wraps is average, more wraps make a thicker tassel. With a threaded needle, pull a long doubled strand of yarn between yarn and template, and slide it up to end. Tie tightly around strands, leaving long ends.

2 Insert scissors at the base of the wraps and cut across all strands. Remove the template.

3 Wrap another strand of yarn tightly around the top a short distance below the head, then tie securely and sew the ends through the wraps and into the tassel head a few times.

4 Trim the ends of the tassel and sew to project with remaining long strand at head. Light pressing or steaming at the end of step 2 makes the tassel sleeker.

FRINGE

1 Cut a cardboard template a little wider than the fringe length. Wind yarn around the cardboard. Cut along one side of the cardboard, making lengths of yarn double its width.

2 Take several lengths (more make a thicker fringe), fold in half and hold the folded loop in front of fabric edge. Insert a crochet hook through back of fabric close to edge or through specially made selvage holes. Catch the folded loop and pull it through to back.

3 Catch strands in hook again and pull through the first loop. Repeat along edge, spacing as required. Trim ends evenly. Fringes can be beaded, knotted, or worked in silky or contrast colored yarns.

DRAWTHREAD BOBBLE

1 Using smaller needles than normal for yarn, cast on five stitches using backward loop cast-on (see p. 35). Work a number of rows in garter or stockinette stitch as desired. Finish with wrong side facing, and slip all the stitches, one by one, over the first one.

2 Cut yarn leaving an 8in (20cm) tail and pull through the remaining stitch. Sew a running stitch with yarn tail around the edge, and pull tightly. (Contrast yarn has been used here for clarity.)

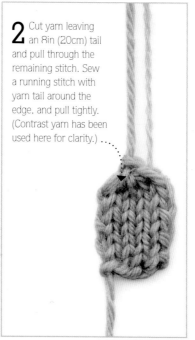

3 Sew together to secure and use the same thread to attach to the project.

COVERED BUTTONS

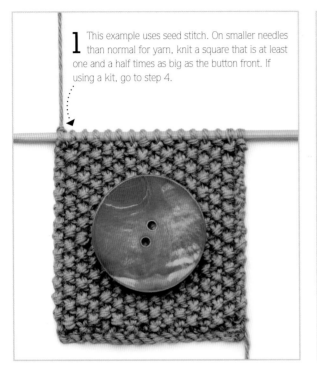

1 This example uses seed stitch. On smaller needles than normal for yarn, knit a square that is at least one and a half times as big as the button front. If using a kit, go to step 4.

2 Cut the yarn with an 8in (20cm) tail, thread a large-eyed needle with the tail and thread back through stitches as they are removed from the needle. Sew small running stitches around the three edges of the knitting, leave the thread end loose. (A contrast thread has been used here for clarity.)

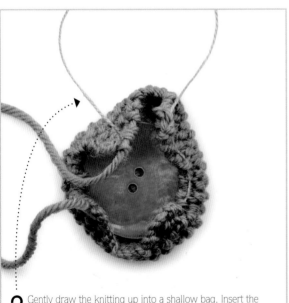

3 Gently draw the knitting up into a shallow bag. Insert the button into the bag and draw the threads tight. Sew closed with yarn end. Sew to garment with knitting yarn or matching thread. To secure big buttons, try sewing through a small plastic button at the back of the knitting at the same time.

4 If using a kit, cast off the square, and follow the manufacturer's instructions to complete the button. A layer of fine woven fabric can be inserted under the knitting to prevent the button from showing through the stretched stitches.

Projects

Striped scarf

This vibrant scarf is an enjoyable, simple way to build up your knitting rhythm and skills. In a simple knit 1, purl 1 rib (also known as a 1 x 1 rib), it involves frequent color changes that make it seem as though the knitting is growing quickly. The rib is double-sided and will not curl, producing a neatly knitted scarf. To trim, add tassels in your choice of remaining yarn.

DIFFICULTY LEVEL
Easy

SIZE
71in (180cm) or desired length

YARN
Rowan Pure Wool DK 50g

A 2   B 3   C 1   D 2   E 1 ball

NEEDLES

A
B

A: 1 pair of US6 (UK8/4mm) needles
B: 1 pair of US3 (UK10/3.25mm) needles

GAUGE
22sts and 30 rows to 4in (10cm) over st st on US6 (UK8/4mm) needles.

PATTERN
Using US3 (UK10/3.25mm) needles and yarn A, cast on 50sts. Change to US6 (UK8/4mm) needles and cont as follows:
Row 1 (RS): S1p, p1, [k1, p1] to end.
Row 2: S1p, p1, [k1, p1] to end.
These 2 rows form a 1 x 1 rib with a slipped stitch at the beginning of each row.
Repeat these 2 rows six times more (14 rows worked in total), ending with a WS row.
Join in yarn B using a slipknot and work another 14 row stripe.
Work 14 row stripes of rib in the following color sequence C, B, A, D, E, D, A, B.
Repeat four times.

To finish stripe sequence, work 14-row stripes in color C, B, then A. Cast off in rib. Cut yarn B (or your choice of yarn) into lengths approximately 9in (22cm) long. Attach these as tassels along each end of the scarf using the method shown on p.170.

COLOR CHANGES Darn ends up the side of the scarf to prevent unsightly ridges from forming (see p. 63). The stripes will remain cleanly divided, without uneven lines or puckering.

TASSELS Leave short gaps to prevent the knots from warping the edge of the scarf and pulling it out of shape. The gaps should be made slightly larger according to the number of strands in the tassels.

SCARF EDGE Slipped stitches at the beginning of each row, referred to as a chain selvage (see p. 135), create a neat and professional-looking edge to the scarf.

Striped hat

This quick and simple beanie can be made to match the Striped scarf on p. 174, and is a recommended project to follow on from a basic strip or square. You use a smaller knitting needle for the ribbed edge, and use the knit two together (k2tog) decreasing technique to shape the top of the hat. The hat is knitted flat and then sewn up with a hidden mattress stitch seam (see p. 149): try to keep the stripes aligned for an especially neat finish.

DIFFICULTY LEVEL
Easy

SIZE
To fit an adult female

YARN
Rowan Pure Wool DK 50g

A 1   B 1   C 1   D 1   E 1 ball

NEEDLES
A: 1 pair of US3 (UK10/3.25mm) needles
B: 1 pair of US6 (UK8/4mm) needles

A

B

GAUGE
22sts and 30 rows to 4in (10cm) over st st on US6 (UK8/4mm) needles

PATTERN
Using US3 (UK10/3.25mm) needles and yarn A, cast on 122 stitches.
Row 1: K2 [p2 k2] to end.
Row 2: P2 [k2 p2] to end
Repeat these 2 rows four times more, decreasing one stitch at end of last row. (121sts)
Change to US6 (UK8/4mm) needles and yarn B.
Work in st st for 8 rows, ending with a WS row. Working all color changes using the alternative method on page 63. Work 8-row stripes in the following sequence: C, B, A. Change to yarn D and work 4 rows st st.

SHAPE CROWN
Row 1: [K10, k2tog] to last st, k1. (111sts)
Row 2 and all foll alt rows: P.
Row 3: K.
Row 5: Change to yarn E. [K9, k2tog] to last st, k1. (101sts)
Row 7: [K8, k2tog] to last st, k1. (91sts)
Row 9: [K7, k2tog] to last st, k1. (81sts)
Row 11: [K6, k2tog] to last st, k1. (71sts)
Row 13: Change to yarn D. [K5, k2tog] to last st, k1. (61sts)
Row 15: [K4, k2tog] to last st, k1. (51sts)
Row 17: [K3, k2tog] to last st, k1. (41sts)
Row 19: [K2, k2tog] to last st, k1. (31sts)
Row 21: Change to yarn A. [K1, k2tog] to last st, k1. (21sts)
Row 23: [K2tog] to last st, k1. (11sts)
Draw yarn through rem stitches and join side seam using mattress stitch (see p. 149).

ELASTICATED EDGE Areas that must fit well, such as hat bands and sleeve cuffs, use stretchy rib stitch (see p. 60) knitted in a smaller needle size for a tight knit and elasticity.

FINISHING THE CROWN For a secure join, leave a long yarn tail at the end of the last row, draw it through the remaining stitches twice, then use it to sew the seam.

INVISIBLE SEAM Using mattress stitch (see p. 149) to sew the seam, worked with the right side of the work showing, allows you to keep the stripes aligned.

Easy arm warmers

These arm warmers are simply knitted as a flat piece and sewn up afterward. Using knit and purl, the stripes are easily and neatly worked by carrying yarns up the side of the work. We have used an elasticated yarn to help the arm warmers fit more snugly. Always be careful to check your gauge, and change needle sizes where necessary.

DIFFICULTY LEVEL
Easy

SIZE
To fit an adult female

YARN
Rowan Calmer 50g

A 1   B 1 ball

NEEDLES
A: 1 pair of US5 (UK9/3.75mm) needles
B: 1 pair of US7 (UK7/4.5mm) needles

A
B

GAUGE
23sts and 33 rows to 4in (10cm) over st st on US7 (UK7/4.5mm) needles

PATTERN
LEFT ARM WARMER
Using yarn A and US7 (UK7/4.5mm) needles and single cast on method (see p.35) cast on 46sts.
Change to US5 (UK9/3.75mm) needles and starting with a k row, work 10 rows in st st, ending with a WS row.
Change to US7 (UK7/4.5mm) needles and work a further 6 rows in st st, ending with a WS row. Join in yarn B.
Next row (RS): Using yarn B, k1, s1 k1 psso, k to last 3sts, k2tog, k1. (44sts)
Work 9 rows without shaping.
Work 10 rows in yarn A without shaping.
Last 20 rows set stripe patt: 10 rows yarn B, 10 rows yarn A. Cont working stripe patt throughout, at same time dec as set on next

and foll 20th row. (40sts)
Work 9 rows without shaping, ending with a WS row.**

Thumb Gusset
Row 1: (Working in yarn A) [k4, M1] three times, k to end. (43sts)
Row 2 and all foll alt rows: P.
Row 3: K5, M1, k to end. (44sts)
Row 5: K5, M1, k4, M1, k6, M1, k to end. (47sts)
Row 7: K9, M1, k8, M1, k to end. (49sts)
Row 9: K9, M1, k10, M1, k to end. (51sts)
Row 11: Using yarn B, k21 and turn, leaving rem sts unworked. Leaving yarn B hanging, join in yarn A, cast on 2sts and p12. You may leave the unworked stitches on stitch holders if desired. (14 live sts remain)

Thumb
Working on these 14sts only, and starting with a k row, work 8 rows st st.
Change to US5 (UK9/3.75mm) needles and using yarn A, work another 7 rows st st. Cast off loosely using US7 (UK7/4.5mm) needles on WS.
Using yarn B, which is still attached at base of thumb, and US7 (UK7/4.5mm) needles, with RS facing, pick up and k 2sts from thumb cast-on and k to end of row. (41sts)
Next row: P.
Work 10 rows without shaping (8 rows B, 2 rows A).
Change to US5 (UK9/3.75mm) needles, and using A, starting with a k row, work 10 rows st st.
Cast off using US7 (UK7/4.5mm) needles, leaving a long tail of yarn for sewing up.
Darn in all ends and join row ends and thumb seams using mattress stitch (see p. 149).

RIGHT ARM WARMER
Work as given for Left Arm warmer to **.
Thumb Gusset
Row 1: (Working in yarn A) k29, [M1, k4] twice, M1, k to end. (43sts)
Row 2 and all foll alt rows: P.
Row 3: K38, M1, k to end. (44sts)
Row 5: K29, M1, k6, M1, k4, M1, k to end. (47sts)
Row 7: K29, M1, k8, M1, k to end. (49sts)
Row 9: K29, M1, k10, M1, k to end. (51sts)
Row 13: Using yarn B, k41 and turn, leaving rem sts unworked. Leave yarn B hanging, join in yarn A, cast on 2sts and p12. Complete as given for Left Arm warmer from Thumb.

WORKING THE STRIPES Twist the unworked color with the yarn you are working with at the end of even-numbered rows. The unworked color is "stitched" in up the side of the stripe—no multiple ends to darn in.

CURLED EDGES Stockinette stitch curls naturally. We've used a small needle at the cuff and finger edge to help with elasticity but a larger size to cast on and cast off to encourage the curl.

Easy arm warmers **179**

Blue and purple blanket

Blankets knitted on large needles with an appropriately proportioned yarn result in a luxuriously thick and warm fabric. To maximize a blanket's insulating properties, choose a yarn made of animal fibers such as pure wool or the wool and alpaca blend we've used here.

DIFFICULTY LEVEL
Easy

SIZE
40 x 49in (100 x 125cm)

YARN
Gedifra Highland Alpaca 100g

A 4   **B** 5   **C** 6   **D** 2 balls

NEEDLES
1 pair of US17 (12mm) needles

GAUGE
8sts and 12 rows to 4in (10cm) over g st

CHART

A	C	D	B
B	A	B	C
C	B	C	A
A	C	D	B
C	B	C	A

Strip 1	Strip 2	Strip 3	Strip 4

PATTERN
Blanket is constructed of four strips, worked bottom to top, as follows (see chart also):

STRIP 1
Using yarn C and US17 (12mm) needles, cast on 21sts and k 30 rows.
Change to yarn A and work 30 rows.
Change to yarn C and work 30 rows.
Change to yarn B and work 30 rows.
Change to yarn A and work 30 rows.
Strip should measure 49in (125cm). Cast off.

STRIP 2
Using yarn B and US17 (12mm) needles, cast on 21sts and k 30 rows.
Change to yarn C and work 30 rows.
Change to yarn B and work 30 rows.
Change to yarn A and work 30 rows.
Change to yarn C and work 30 rows.
Strip should measure 49in (125cm). Cast off.

STRIP 3
Using yarn C and US17 (12mm) needles, cast on 21sts and k 30 rows.
Change to yarn D and work 30 rows.
Change to yarn C and work 30 rows.
Change to yarn B and work 30 rows.
Change to yarn D and work 30 rows.
Strip should measure 49in (125cm). Cast off.

STRIP 4
Using yarn A and US17 (12mm) needles, cast on 21sts and k 30 rows.
Change to yarn B and work 30 rows.
Change to yarn A and work 30 rows.
Change to yarn C and work 30 rows.
Change to yarn B and work 30 rows.
Strip should measure 49in (125cm). Cast off.

FINISHING
Lay the strips alongside each other and match cast-on and cast-off edges. Sew up, with WS facing, using whipstitch (see p. 151). Block and darn in all ends.

Attach one tassel to each corner of the blanket (6in/15cm long and made of three strands of yarn).

WHIPSTITCH STRIPS It is best to whipstitch (see p. 151) garter stitch strips, since this blends with the ridged texture of the knitted fabric. It also doesn't form a reverse-side seam, making the blanket more attractive.

GARTER STITCH (see p. 59) is easy and is identical on both sides, which prevents the knitted fabric from curling, so little blocking is required. Perfect for hand-knitted blankets.

Blue and purple blanket

Baby's cardigan

This soft, luxurious cardigan is perfect for a newborn. You only need to know stockinette stitch for the body and garter stitch for the stylized yoke and sleeves. Boys' and girls' buttonholes appear on different sides, so follow the relevant instructions below.

DIFFICULTY LEVEL
Easy

SIZE
To fit a newborn baby

YARN
Rowan Pure Cashmere DK 25g

x 3 balls

NEEDLES
1 pair of US3 (UK10/3.25mm) needles

NOTIONS
1 button

GAUGE
27sts and 37 rows to 4in (10cm) over st st using US3 (UK10/3.25mm) needles

PATTERN
Using cable cast-on method (see p.37), cast on 62sts.
Row 1 (WS): K.
Rows 2 and 3: As row 1.
Row 4 (RS): K.
Row 5: P.
Last 2 rows set st st. Continue working in st st until work measures 6¾in (17cm) from cast-on edge, ending with a WS row.

SHAPE ARMS
Next 2 rows: Cast on 36sts knit to end. (134sts)
Cont in g st as set for a further 32 rows.

SHAPE RIGHT FRONT
Next row: K57 and turn, leaving rem 77sts on a holder.

SHAPE NECK
Row 1 (WS): K1, s1 k1 psso, k to end. (56sts)
Row 2 (RS): K to last 3sts, k2tog, k1. (55sts)
Row 3: As row 1. (54sts)
Knit 11 rows ending with a RS row.
Inc row (WS): K1, M1, k to end. (55sts)
Knit 3 rows without shaping.
Cont increasing at neck edge as set by inc row on next and foll 3 alt rows, then at neck edge of foll 2 rows. (61sts)
Next row: Cast on and k 7sts, k to end. (68sts)

For a Girl Only:
Place buttonhole: K to last 5sts, cast off 3sts, k1.
Next row: K2, cast on 3sts, k to end.

For a Boy Only:
Knit 2 rows.

For Boy and Girl:
Shape underarm (RS): Cast off 36sts, k to end.
Row 1 (WS): K5, p to end.
Row 2 (RS): Knit to end.
Last 2 rows set st st with g st border.
Rep last 2 rows until work measures 6¼in (16cm) from underarm, ending with a RS row.
Knit 3 rows, cast off.

LEFT FRONT
With RS facing, rejoin yarn to rem sts.
Cast off next 20 sts, k to end. (57sts)
Row 1 (WS): K to last 3sts, k2tog, k1. (56sts)
Row 2 (RS): K1, s1, k1, psso, k to end. (55sts)
Row 3(WS): As row 1. (54sts)
Knit 12 rows without shaping, ending with a WS row.

Inc row (RS): K1, M1, k to end. (55sts)
Knit 2 rows without shaping.
Cont increasing at neck edge as set by inc row on next and foll 3 alt rows, then at neck edge of foll 2 rows. (61sts)
Next row (WS): K.
Next row (RS): Cast on and k 7sts, k to end. (68sts)

For a Girl Only:
Knit 2 rows

For a Boy Only:
Place buttonhole: K to last 5sts, cast off 3sts, k1.
Next row: K2, cast on 3sts, k to end.

For Boy and Girl:
Shape underarm (WS): Cast off 36sts, k to end.
Row 1 (RS): Knit to end.
Row 2 (WS): P to last 5 sts, k5.
Rep last 2 rows until work measure 6¼in (16cm) from underarm ending with a RS row.
Knit 3 rows. Cast off.
Join side and underarm seams using mattress stitch (see p.149).
Steam gently and attach button.

GARTER STITCH Using garter stitch makes a thick fabric (see p.59). It is used here on the arms to help keep the baby warm, and also to provide a variation in texture.

STOCKINETTE STITCH This stitch uses only basic knits and purls, and works well in this yarn as it produces a professional and taut fabric that looks store-bought. (see p.59)

BUTTONS A professional finish can be achieved with the right trimmings and embellishments. This understated shell button has flashes of many colors and will blend with anything.

Baby's cardigan **183**

Baby's first hat

This hat is designed to match the Baby's cardigan on p. 182. It is sized to fit a newborn baby, but can be made bigger by using a thicker yarn with the appropriate needles. For example, try a different double-knit yarn with US6 (UK8/4mm) needles to make a hat for a baby 3–6 months in age. A tiny hat like this is very quick to knit. We have chosen cashmere for its warmth and buttery softness, but another very soft easy-care yarn would make an ideal substitute.

DIFFICULTY LEVEL
Easy

SIZE
To fit a newborn baby

YARN
Rowan Pure Cashmere DK 25g

x 1 ball

NEEDLES
1 pair of US3 (UK10/3.25mm) needles

GAUGE
25sts and 34 rows to 4in (10cm) over st st.

SPECIAL ABBREVIATIONS
rib Work in rib, knitting all presented knit stitches and purling all presented purl stitches.
rib2tog Working in rib, k2tog.

PATTERN
Cast on 83sts using cable cast-on method (see p. 37).
Row 1 (RS): *K1, p1, rep from * to last st, k1.
Row 2: *P1, k1, rep from * to last st, p1.
Rep last 2 rows once more.
Row 5: [Rib 13, rib2tog] five times, rib to end. (78sts)
Next row: P.
Next row: K.
These 2 rows form st st.
Work in st st for another 17 rows.

SHAPE CROWN
Row 1 (RS): [K6, k2tog] nine times, k to end. (69sts)
Row 2 and every foll alt row: P.
Row 3: K.
Row 5: [K5, k2tog] nine times, k to end. (60sts)
Row 7: [K4, k2tog] nine times, k to end. (51sts)
Row 9: [K3, k2tog] ten times, k to end. (41sts)
Row 11: [K2, k2tog] ten times, k to end. (31sts)
Row 13: [K1, k2tog] ten times, k to end. (21sts)
Row 15: [K2tog] ten times, k1. (11sts)
Break off yarn leaving a long tail and draw this through rem sts twice. Use this end to join row ends using mattress stitch. Steam lightly.

TIGHTLY KNITTED FABRIC A tightly knitted fabric is created by using smaller needles than those specified on the yarn label. The tight fabric keeps heat from escaping.

SOFT RIBBING This dainty cap sits against the baby's head, holding its shape with soft ribbing that is just snug enough to retain warmth. By using the same needles throughout for the hat, the ribbing does not end up too tight.

SEAM With babies' garments, it is important not to add extra bulk with chunky seams. Use mattress stitch (see p. 149) for a neat hidden seam.

TOP OF CROWN By tightly pulling the yarn through the stitches twice at the top of the hat, you will prevent gaps from forming in the future. Loosely gathered stitches may slide apart over time as a result of wear and tear.

Baby's booties

As with the heel of a sock, these booties need to curve to fit a very irregular shape—a baby's foot. To achieve a good fit, we use increases and decreases to push the curvature of the work in the right direction. We've chosen a DK yarn and used smaller than recommended needles to achieve a taut, firm fabric suitable for these tiny shoes.

DIFFICULTY LEVEL
Moderate

SIZE
To fit a baby aged 0–6 months

YARN
Rowan Lenpur Linen 50g

x 1 ball

NEEDLES
A: 1 pair of US2 (UK12/2.75mm) needles
B: 1 pair of US3 (UK11/3mm) needles

A
B

NOTIONS
28in (70cm) matching ribbon, ¼–⅜in (5–7mm) wide

GAUGE
25sts and 46 rows to 4in (10cm) over g st using US2 (UK11/3mm) needles

PATTERN
BOOTIES (Make 2)
Using US3 (UK11/3mm) needles, cast on 37sts.
Row 1 (WS): K.
Row 2: Inc in next st, k15, inc in next st, k3, inc in next st, k15, inc in last st. (41sts)
Row 3 and all foll alt rows: K.
Row 4: Inc in next st, k17, inc in next st, k3, inc in next st, k17, inc in last st. (45sts)
Row 6: Inc in next st, k19, inc in next st, k3, inc in next st, k19, inc in last st. (49sts)
K 16 rows, ending with a WS row.

Shape for Toe
Row 1 (RS): K17, s1 k1 psso, k11, k2tog, k17. (47sts)
Row 2: K17, s1 k1 psso, k9, k2tog, k17. (45sts)
Row 3: K17, s1 k1 psso, k7, k2tog, k17. (43sts)
Row 4: K17, s1 k1 psso, k5, k2tog, k17. (41sts)
Row 5: K17, s1 k1 psso, k3, k2tog, k17. (39sts)
Row 7: K17, s1 k1 psso, k1, k2tog, k17. (37sts)
Row 8: K17, s1 k2tog psso, k17. (35sts)

Shape for Ankle
Using US2 (UK12/2.75mm) needles and work as foll:
Next row (RS): K1, *p1, k1, rep from * to end.
Next row: P1, *k1, p1, rep from * to end. Rep last 2 rows twice more.
Eyelet row: K1, *yo, k2tog, rep from * to end.
Next row: P1, *k1, p1, rep from * to end.

Work Edging
Next row: (Casting off) *k2, pass first st over second so that one st remains on right-hand needle as if casting off, place this one st back on left-hand needle, rep from * until one st remains. Fasten off, leaving a long tail of yarn.

Join row ends with mattress stitch (see p. 149), using long tail of yarn from cast-off edge. Fold over ribbed edging and catch to main bootie with a long running stitch (see p. 167). Thread ribbon through eyelets and tie in a bow.

TOE SHAPING Increases and decreases, at regular points in the rows, shape the toe. They are hidden behind the ridges of the garter stitch, giving the bootie a completely smooth appearance.

ANKLE CUFF The cuff is knitted as a long piece, then folded and stitched to create a casing for the ribbon. The cast-off adds a wavy edge to the design.

OVERSEWN SEAMS These garter stitch booties have a whipstitched seam (see p. 151). This will sit completely flat and not form an uncomfortable, bulky seam on the right or wrong side of the work.

Baby's booties 187

Men's gloves

To make these gloves, you will be working M1 increases (see p. 71), dividing stitches, and working on part of a row at a time to form long strips of fabric for the fingers. The organic wool used still contains some lanolin, making it durable and slightly waterproof.

DIFFICULTY LEVEL
Moderate

SIZE
To fit an adult male

YARN
Rowan British Sheep Breeds DK
Undyed 50g

x 2 balls

NEEDLES
A: 1 pair of US3 (UK10/3.25mm) needles
B: 1 pair of US5 (UK9/3.75mm) needles

A
B

GAUGE
24sts and 30 rows to 4in (10cm) over stockinette stitch using US5 (UK9/3.75mm) needles

PATTERN
LEFT HAND
Using US3 (UK10/3.25mm) needles and double cast-on method (see p. 39), cast on 45sts.
Row 1 (RS): K1, *p1, k1 tbl, rep from * to end.
Row 2: *P1 tbl, k1, rep from * to end.
These two rows set twisted rib.
Rep last 2 rows until work measures 2½in (6.5cm), ending with a RS row.
Next row (WS): Rib 7, M1, [rib 8, M1] four times, patt to end. (50sts)
Change to US5 (UK9/3.75mm) needles and work in st st for 6 rows, ending on a WS row.
Thumb
Row 1 (RS): K22, M1, k3, M1, k to end. (52sts)

Starting with a p row, work 3 rows st st.
Row 5: K22, M1, k5, M1, k to end. (54sts)
Row 6 and all foll alt rows: P.
Row 7: K22, M1, k7, M1, k to end. (56sts)
Row 9: K22, M1, k9, M1, k to end. (58sts)
Row 11: K22, M1, k11, M1, k to end. (60sts)
Row 13: K22, M1, k13, M1, k to end. (62sts)
Row 15: K22, M1, k15, M1, k to end. (64sts)
Row 16: P.
Row 17: K39. Turn.
Row 18: P17. Turn.
Working on these 17sts only, work 19 rows st st ending with a RS row.
**Next row: P1, [p2tog] eight times. (9sts)
Leaving a long tail, break yarn and thread through rem sts.
Rejoin yarn at base of thumb and k to end.
Starting with a p row, work 13 rows st st without shaping.
First Finger
Next row: K30. Turn.
Next row: P13. Turn, cast on 2sts. (15sts for finger)
Working on these 15sts only, work 24 rows st st.
Next row: K1, [k2tog] seven times. (8sts)
Leaving a long tail, break yarn and thread through rem sts.
Second Finger
With RS facing, pick up and knit 2sts from base of first finger, k6. Turn.
Next row: P14. Turn and cast on 2sts. (16sts for second finger)
Working on these 16sts only, work 24 rows st st.
Next row: [K2tog] eight times.
Leaving a long tail, break yarn and thread through rem sts.
Third Finger
With RS facing, pick up and knit 2sts from base of first finger, k6. Turn.
Next row: P14. Turn and cast on 2sts. (16sts

for third finger)
Working on these 16sts only, work 22 rows st st.
Next row: [K2tog] eight times.
Leaving a long tail, break yarn and thread through rem sts.
Fourth Finger
With RS facing, pick up and knit 2sts from base of first finger, k5. Turn.
Next row: P12. Turn and cast on 2sts. (14sts for fourth finger)
Working on these 14sts only, work 15 rows st st.
Next row (WS): [P2tog] seven times.
Leaving a long tail, break yarn and thread through rem sts.
Use all long tails of yarn to sew up corresponding finger using mattress stitch, being especially careful to run as fine a seam as possible. Continue fourth finger seam to cuff. Block according to instructions on yarn, but do not block rib.

RIGHT HAND
Work as for left-hand glove up to Thumb.
Thumb
Row 1 (RS): K25, M1, k3, M1, k to end. (52sts)
Starting with a p row, work 3 rows st st.
Row 5: K25, M1, k5, M1, k to end. (54sts)
Row 6 and all foll alt rows: P.
Row 7: K25, M1, k7, M1, k to end. (56sts)
Row 9: K25, M1, k9, M1, k to end. (58sts)
Row 11: K25, M1, k11, M1, k to end. (60sts)
Row 13: K25, M1, k13, M1, k to end. (62sts)
Row 15: K25, M1, k15, M1, k to end. (64sts)
Row 16: P.
Row 17: K42. Turn.
Row 18: P17. Turn.
Working on these 17sts only, work 19 rows st st ending with a RS row.
Work from ** to end of instructions for the left-hand glove.

FINGERTIPS Drawing the yarn through the remaining stitches to finish encourages the area of work to curve, which is perfect for creating fingertips.

RIBBED CUFF Twisted stitches, like cables, tighten a knitted fabric and make a more elasticated wrist. Blocking ribbing can loosen it and is not advised.

Men's gloves **189**

Ankle socks

These thick, cozy socks are quick to knit and made from a machine-washable wool blend. They have a reinforced heel, which is worked as a short flap, and then on the following rounds you pick up stitches along the edge of the flap to turn the heel.

DIFFICULTY LEVEL
Moderate

SIZE
To fit an adult female, shoe size UK 5–8

YARN
Gedifra Riana Color 50g

x 2 balls

NEEDLES
4 x US7 (UK7/4.5mm) double-pointed needles

GAUGE
19sts and 25 rows to 4in (10cm) over st st

PATTERN
(Make 2)
CUFF
Using the double cast-on method (see p. 39), cast on 40sts.
Divide sts between three needles and arrange as foll:
Needle 1: 10 heel sts.
Needle 2: 20 instep sts.
Needle 3: 10 heel sts.
Next round: [K1 tbl, p1] to end of round.
Last row sets twisted rib. Work in this patt as set for another 9 rows.

LEG
Work in stockinette stitch (k every round) until work measures 5½in (13cm).

DIVIDE FOR HEEL
K10, turn.
S1 purlwise, p19 on to same dpn. Divide remaining 20sts between two dpn.
With RS facing, work back and forth as follows:

Row 1: *S1 purlwise, k1. Repeat from * to end.
Row 2: S1 purlwise, p to end.
Repeat these 2 rows three more times (8 rows worked in total).

TURN HEEL
Row 1 (RS): K11, s1 k1 psso, k1. Turn.
Row 2 (WS): S1, p4, p2tog, p1. Turn.
Row 3: S1, k5, s1 k1 psso, k1. Turn.
Row 4: S1, p6, p2tog, p1. Turn.
Row 5: S1, k7, s1 k1 psso, k1. Turn.
Row 6: S1, p8, p2tog, p1. Turn.
Row 7: S1, k9, s1 k1 psso, k1. Turn.
Row 9: S1, p10, p2tog. Turn.
12sts remain. K6.

HEEL GUSSET
Rearrange sts on needles 2 and 3 so they now sit on the same needle. One needle is now spare. Use this spare needle to knit across the remaining 6 heel sts.
Continuing with the same needle, pick up 6sts along the side of the heel, pick up a loop of yarn to M1 from between instep and heel sts (needle 1 has 13sts in total).
On next needle, k across 20 instep sts (needle 2).
With free needle, pick up and knit from row below the first heel st to M1.
With same needle, pick up 6sts along side of the heel and work across remaining heel sts (needle 3 has 13sts in total).
Shape Gusset
Round 1: (Dec round.)
Needle 1: K to 3sts from end. K2tog, k1.
Needle 2: (Instep.) Work even.
Needle 3: K1, s1 k1 psso, work to end.
Round 2: K.
Repeat rounds 1 and 2 twice more. (40sts)

FOOT
Continue working in rounds until foot measures 8in (20cm) from base of heel.

SHAPE TOE
Round 1: Work to last 3sts on needle 1, k2tog, k1. On Needle 2, k1, ssk, work to last 3sts, k2tog, k1. On Needle 3, k1, ssk, complete round.
Round 2: Work even.
Repeat rounds 1 and 2 until 28sts remain in total. Work round 1 only until 12sts remain (6 instep sts, 6 sole sts).

FINISHING
K across sts on needle 1. Turn sock inside out through the middle of the needles. Slip sts from needle 3 to opposite end of needle 1. Holding two needles together, and with WS facing, cast off using three-needle cast-off (see p. 52).
Darn in ends.
Work second sock.

SLIPPED STITCH HEEL By slipping stitches at the heel, you line the inside of the sock with strands of yarn, making the area stronger, which is important when a soft fiber is used.

DOUBLE CAST-ON A sock cuff is constantly being stretched, so it's a good idea to use a strong cast-on. The double cast-on (see p. 39) is ideal, as the cuff is reinforced with an extra strand of yarn when worked.

Raglan sweater

This is a great sweater for a beginner who wants to make their first garment. It is knitted with a chunky yarn on large needles so it will be quick to finish. It uses basic knitting stitches such as stockinette stitch and rib, as well as introducing additional techniques such as picking up stitches and decreasing. The sweater can be made in three sizes.

DIFFICULTY LEVEL
Moderate

SIZE
Adult unisex 38 (42, 46) in [96.5 (107, 117) cm].

YARN
Wendy Merino Chunky 50g

x 14 balls (16, 18)

NEEDLES

A

B

A: 1 pair of US10 (UK4/6mm) needles
B: 1 pair of US10½ (UK3/6.5mm) needles
4 stitch holders

GAUGE
15sts and 20 rows to 4in (10cm) over st st on US10½ (UK3/6.5mm) needles

PATTERN
BACK
Using US10 (UK4/6mm) needles cast on 76 (84, 90) sts using knit-on cast on (see p. 36).
Ribbing
Row 1: K1 (1,0) * k2, p2 * to last 3 (3,2) stitches, k3 (3,2).
Row 2: P3 (3,2) * k2, p2 * to last st, p1 (1,0).
Rep these 2 rows 5 more times or until work measures 3in, ending with a WS row.
Change to US10½ (UK3/6.5mm) needles and beg with a k row start knitting in st st until the knitting measures 17½ (18, 19) in

(44 (46, 48) cm) from the cast on edge, ending with a WS row.

RAGLAN ARMHOLE SHAPING
RS facing. Cast off 3sts at the beg of the next 2 rows. 70 (78, 84) sts.
Dec 1 st at each end of next 4 rows. 62 (70, 76) sts
Next row (RS): K2, sl1, k1, psso, k to last 4 st, k2tog, k2.
Next row: Purl.
Rep the last 2 rows, dec as set on each RS row until 22 (24, 26) sts rem. Make sure the last p row is worked.
Slip rem st onto a stitch holder (see p. 50).

FRONT
Work the same as the back until there are 36sts left after the start of the raglan armhole shaping, ending with a WS row.

LEFT FRONT RAGLAN AND NECK SHAPING
Next row (RS): K2, sl1, k1, psso, k10, slip rem 22sts from the left needle on to a stitch holder.
Turn the knitting so WS is facing and working only on the 13 st left.
Next row (WS): P2tog, p to end. (12 sts)
Next row (RS): K2, sl1, k1, psso, k to last 2 sts, k2tog.
Next row (WS): Purl. Rep these two row 3 times (4 sts).
Next row (RS): K2, sl1, k1, psso (3sts)
Next row (WS): P2tog, p1. (2sts)
Next row (RS): K2tog (1st)
Cut yarn, leaving at least an 8in (20cm) long tail. Pass through the remaining stitch to secure.

RIGHT FRONT RAGLAN AND NECK SHAPING
Leaving the central 8 st on the holder, slip the 14sts for the right side of the neck back onto

a needle.
Rejoin yarn at center, k to to the last 4sts, k2tog, k2 (13sts).
Next row (WS): P11, p2tog (12sts)
Next row (RS): K2tog, k to last 4sts, k2tog, k2 (10sts)
Next row: Purl.
Next row: K2tog, k to last 4 sts, k2tog, k2 (8sts)
Next row: Purl.
Next row: K2tog, k to last 4 sts, k2tog, k2 (6sts)
Next row: Purl.
Next row: K2tog twice, k2 (4st)
Next row: Purl.
Next row: K2tog, k2 (3st)
Next row: P1, p2tog (2st)
Next row: K2tog (1st)
Cut the yarn, leaving at least an 8in (20cm) long tail. Pull through the remaining stitch to fasten.

SLEEVES
Work two the same.
Cast on 32 (36, 40) sts using US10 (UK4/6mm) needles and knit-on cast on.
Ribbing
Row 1 (RS): K1, *k2, p2 * to last 3sts, k3
Row 2 (WS): P3, * k2, p2 * to last st, p1
Rep these 2 rows 5 more times.
Change to US10½ (UK3/6.5mm) needles and cont in st st with the first row as follows:
Next row (INC) (RS): Kfb, k7 (8,9), kfb, K7 (8,9), kfb, k7 (8,9), kfb, k7 (8,9), kfb. 37 (41, 45) sts
Next row (WS): Purl
Next row: Knit
Next row: Purl
Next row (INC) (RS): Kfb, k to last 2 sts, kfb, k1. Work 5 rows in st st, ending with a WS row.
Rep these 6 rows, inc as described until there are 63 (67, 71) sts. All incs should be

worked on RS rows.

Once there are 63 (67, 71) sts cont in st st until the sleeve measures 18 (19, 20) in (46 (48, 50) cm) from the cast on edge, ending with a WS row.

SHAPE TOP OF RAGLAN SLEEVES

Cast off 3 stitches as the beg of the next 2 rows 56 (61, 65) sts

Decrease (using k2tog/p2tog) 1 st at each end of the next 4 rows 48 (53, 57) sts

Next row (RS): K2, sl1, k1, psso, k to last 4 sts, k2tog, k2. 46 (51, 55) sts

Next row (WS): Purl

Rep these 2 rows, dec on every RS row until 9sts remain.

Slip rem 9sts on to a stitch holder.

Join pieces together

Sew both sleeves to the front, and the right sleeve to the back, leaving the seam between the back and the left sleeve open. (The right and left is determined as it would be worn). Use mattress stitch to join the seams.

NECKBAND

Using US10 (UK4/6mm) needles and with the RS of the sweater facing, rejoin yarn and knit across the 9sts from the stitch holder at the top of the left sleeve.

Next, pick up and knit 8sts down the left side of front of neck.

Knit 8sts from the front stitch holder.

Pick up and knit 8sts up the right side of the front neck.

Knit 9sts from the stitch holder at the top of right shoulder.

Knit 22 (24, 26) sts from the back stitch holder. 64 (66, 68) sts

Next row (WS): P2, kfb p2 *k2, p2* to last 3 sts, inc in next st, p2. 66 (70) sts

Work 4 rows in k2, p2 rib as set by this last row.

Next row (RS): Cast off in rib patt, making sure the cast off is not tight. It must be stretchy enough for the sweater to fit over the wearer's head.

Join the pieces together

Sew the edges of the neckband together using mattress stitch. Sew left raglan seam in place. Sew side seams and sleeve seams together using mattress stitch.

RIB STITCH Start jumper at the bottom using double rib stitch. This stitch, which is also used for the cuffs and neckband, is worked on smaller sized needles to make a tighter stitch and improve elasticity.

Stitch patterns

Stitch patterns

These swatches demonstrate how the techniques on pp. 30–171 can be turned into interesting and original knitted fabrics. Even if you are new to knitting, you have probably already heard of some of the well-known stitches, such as stockinette and seed, but what you might not know is that there are many, many alternatives, creating any number of attractive effects, from striking cables and colorwork to delicate beading. Take a look through this chapter to establish the kinds of effects that appeal to you. From there you can find the relevant techniques in the Techniques chapter on pp. 30–171.

Knit and purl stitch patterns

Here are a few of the vast array of stitch patterns created by combining knit and purl stitches. Each one produces a flat, reversible knitted fabric and is simple to work. Those that have no specific right side (RS) look exactly the same on both the front and the back, and the few with a marked right side have an attractive texture on the wrong side as well. Because the edges of these stitches do not curl, they are ideal for making simple scarves, baby blankets, and throws. See pp. 57–60 for step-by-step guidance on knit and purl stitches.

SEED STITCH

INSTRUCTIONS
Cast on an even number of sts.
Row 1: *K1, p1, rep from *.
Row 2: *P1, k1, rep from *.
Rep rows 1 and 2 to form patt.

DOUBLE RIB

INSTRUCTIONS
Cast on a multiple of 4sts.
Row 1: *K2, p2, rep from *.
Rep row 1 to form patt.

SINGLE RIB

INSTRUCTIONS
Cast on a multiple of 2sts.
Row 1: *K1, p1, rep from * to end.
Row 2: As row 1.
Rep rows 1 and 2 to form patt.

ENGLISH RIB

INSTRUCTIONS
Cast on an odd number of sts.
Row 1: S1, *p1, k1, rep from * to end.
Row 2: S1, *k1b, p1, rep from * to end.
Rep rows 1 and 2 to form patt.

FISHERMAN'S RIB

INSTRUCTIONS
Cast on an odd number of sts
and knit 1 row.
Row 1 (RS): S1, *k1b, p1, rep
from * to end.
Row 2: S1, *p1, k1b, rep from *
to last 2sts, p1, k1.
Rep rows 1 and 2 to form patt.

MOCK RIB STITCH

INSTRUCTIONS
Cast on an odd number of sts.
Row 1 (RS): *P1, k1, rep from *
to last st, k1.
Row 2: K.
Rep rows 1 and 2 to form patt.

MOSS STITCH

INSTRUCTIONS
Cast on an odd number of sts.
Row 1 (RS): *K1, p1, rep from *
to last st, k1.
Row 2: *P1, k1, rep from * to
last st, p1.
Row 3: As row 2.
Row 4: As row 1.
Rep rows 1–4 to form patt.

BROKEN SEED STITCH

INSTRUCTIONS
Cast on an odd number of sts.
Row 1 (RS): K.
Row 2: *P1, k1, rep from * to
last st, k1.
Rep rows 1 and 2 to form patt.

BASKETWEAVE STITCH

INSTRUCTIONS
Cast on a multiple of 8sts.
Rows 1–5: *K4, p4, rep
from *.
Rows 6–10: *P4, k4, rep
from *.
Rep rows 1–10 to form patt.

GARTER RIB

INSTRUCTIONS
Cast on a multiple of 8sts plus
4 extra sts.
Row 1 (RS): K4, *p4, k4, rep
from * to end.
Row 2: P.
Rep rows 1 and 2 to form patt.

TRAVELING RIB

INSTRUCTIONS
Cast on a multiple of 4sts.
Row 1 (RS): *K2, p2, rep from * to end.
Row 2: As row 1.
Row 3: *K1, p2, k1, rep from * to end.
Row 4: *P1, k2, p1, rep from * to end.
Row 5: *P2, k2, rep from * to end.
Row 6: As row 5.

Row 7: As row 4.
Row 8: As row 3.
Rep rows 1–8 to form patt.

STRIPED BOX STITCH

INSTRUCTIONS

Cast on a multiple of 6sts plus 3 extra sts.

Row 1 and all odd-numbered rows (RS): K.

Row 2: K.

Rows 4 and 6: P3, *k3, p3, rep from *.

Rows 8 and 10: K.

Rows 12 and 14: K3, *p3, k3, rep from *.

Row 16: K.

Rep rows 1–16 to form patt.

STOCKINETTE BOX STITCH

INSTRUCTIONS

Cast on a multiple of 10sts plus 5 extra sts.

Row 1: *K5, p5, rep from * to last 5sts, k5.

Row 2: P.

Repeat last 2 rows twice more, then row 1 again.

Row 8: K5, *p5, k5, rep from * to end.

Row 9: K.

Repeat last 2 rows twice more, then row 8 again.

DOUBLE SEED STITCH

INSTRUCTIONS

Cast on a multiple of 6sts plus 2 extra sts.

Row 1 (RS): K.

Row 2: K2, *p4, k2, rep from * to end.

Row 3: As row 1.

Row 4: P2, *p1, k2, p3, rep from * to end.

Rep rows 1–4 to form patt.

DIAMOND STITCH

INSTRUCTIONS

Cast on a multiple of 9sts.

Row 1 (RS): K2, *p5, k4, rep from * to last 7sts, p5, k2.

Row 2: P1, *k7, p2, rep from * to last 8sts, k7, p1.

Row 3: P.

Row 4: Rep row 2.

Row 5: Rep row 1.

Row 6: P3, *k3, p6, rep from * to last 6sts, k3, p3.

Row 7: K4, *p1, k8, rep from * to last 5sts, p1, k4.

Row 8: Rep row 6.

Rep rows 1–8 to form patt.

Increasing and decreasing

BASIC CHEVRON

INSTRUCTIONS
Cast on a multiple of 12sts.
Row 1 (RS): *K2tog, k3, [inc in next st] twice, k3, s1 k1 psso, rep from * to end.
Row 2: P.
Rep rows 1 and 2 to form patt.

GARTER CHEVRON

INSTRUCTIONS
Cast on a multiple of 11sts.
Row 1 (WS): K.
Rows 2, 3, 4, and 5: As row 1.
Row 6: *K2tog, k2, [inc in next st] twice, k3, s1 k1 psso, rep from * to end.
Row 7: P.
Rep last 2 rows twice more, then row 6 again.
Rep rows 1–12 to form patt.

DIAGONAL RIB

INSTRUCTIONS
Cast on a multiple of 2sts.
Row 1 (WS): *K1, p1, rep from * to end.
Row 2: S1 p1 psso, *k1, p1, rep from * to last 2sts, k1, [p1, k1] into next st.
Row 3: *P1, k1, rep from * to last 2sts, p2.
Row 4: S1 k1 psso, *p1, k1, rep from * to last 2sts, p1 [k1 p1] into next st.
Rep rows 1–4 to form patt.

BLACKBERRY STITCH

INSTRUCTIONS
Cast on a multiple of 4sts plus 2 extra sts.
Row 1 (RS): P.
Row 2: K1, *[k1, p1, k1] into next st, p3tog, rep from * to last st, k1.
Row 3: P.
Row 4: K1, *p3tog, [k1, p1, k1] into next st, rep from * to last st, k1.
Rep rows 1–4 to form patt.

Cable and twist stitch patterns

KEY

☐ K on RS rows, P on WS rows	◪ T2L	⬛ MB = make bobble
⬤ P on RS rows, K on WS rows	◪ T2R	○ yfwd

◪ k2tog   ◪ ssk   ◪ sl k2tog psso   ◪ s2 K1 p2sso   ◪ CR4L   ◪ CR4R

☒☒ C4B   ☒☒☒ C6B   ☒☒☒☒ C8B   ◪ CR2R

☒☒ C4F   ☒☒☒ C6F   ☒☒☒☒ C8F   ◪ CR2L

WAVY CABLE

INSTRUCTIONS
Special abbreviations
CR2R: Skip first st on left needle and k 2nd st through front of loop (do not drop st off left needle), then p first st on left needle and drop both sts off this needle at same time.
CR2L: Skip first st on left needle and p 2nd st by taking right needle behind first st to do so (so do not drop st off left needle), then k first st on left needle and drop both sts off together.
Cast on a multiple of 3sts (a minimum of 9sts).
Row 1 (RS): *P1, CR2R, rep from * to end.
Row 2: *K1, p1, k1, rep from * to end.
Row 3: *CR2R, p1, rep from * to end.
Row 4: *K2, p1, rep from * to end.
Row 5: *K1, p2, rep from * to end.
Row 6: As row 4.

Row 7: *CR4L, p1, rep from * to end.
Row 8: As row 2.
Row 9: *P1, CR4L, rep from * to end.
Row 10: *P1, k2, rep from * to end.
Row 11: *P2, k1, rep from * to end.
Row 12: As row 10.
Rep rows 1–12 to form patt.

DIAMOND CABLE

INSTRUCTIONS
Special abbreviations
CR4L: Place 2sts on cable needle and leave at front of work, p2 from left needle, then k2 from cable needle.
CR4R: Place 2sts on cable needle and leave at back of work, k2 from left needle, then p2 from cable needle.
C4F: Place 2sts on cable needle and leave at front of work, k2, then k2 from cable needle.

Cast on a multiple of 20sts.
Row 1: *P8, C4F, p8, rep from * to end.
Row 2: *K8, p4, k8, rep from * to end.
Row 3: *P6, CR4R, CR4L, p6, rep from * to end.
Row 4: *K6, p2, k4, p2, k6, rep from * to end.
Row 5: *P4, CR4R, p4, CR4L, p4, rep from * to end.
Row 6: *K4, p2, k8, p2, k4, rep from * to end.
Row 7: *P2, CR4R, p8, CR4L, p2, rep from * to end.
Row 8: *K2, p2, k12, p2, k2, rep from * to end.

Row 9: *P2, CR4L, p8, CR4R, p2, rep from * to end.
Row 10: As row 6.
Row 11: *P4, CR4L, p4, CR4R, p4, rep from * to end.
Row 12: As row 6.
Row 13: *P6, CR4L, CR4R, p6, rep from * to end.
Row 14: As row 2.
Rep rows 1–14 to form patt.

BRAIDED CABLE

INSTRUCTIONS

Special abbreviations

C8F: Place 4sts on cable needle and leave at front of work, k4 from left needle, then k4 from cable needle.

C8B: Place 4sts on cable needle and leave at back of work, k4 from left needle, then k4 from cable needle.

Cast on a multiple of 20sts.

Row 1: *P4, k12, p4, rep from * to end.

Row 2 and all foll alt rows: *K4, p12, k4, rep from * to end.

Row 3: *P4, C8F, k4, p4, rep from * to end.

Rows 5 and 7: As row 1.

Row 9: *P4, k4, C8B, rep from * to end.

Row 11: As row 1.

Row 12: As row 2.

Rep rows 1–12 to form patt.

FOUR-STITCH CABLE PATTERN

INSTRUCTIONS

Special abbreviations

C4F: Slip next 2sts on to cable needle and hold at front of work, k2 from left needle, then k2 from cable needle.

C4B: Slip next 2sts on to cable needle and hold at back of work, k2 from left needle, then k2 from cable needle.

Cast on a multiple of 14sts plus 3 extra sts.

Row 1 (RS): P3, *k4, p3, rep from *.

Row 2: K3, *p4, k3, rep from *.

Row 3: P3, *k4, p3, C4F, p3, rep from *.

Row 4: Rep row 2.

Row 5: P3, *C4B, p3, k4, p3, rep from *.

Rep rows 2–5 to form patt.

HORSESHOE CABLE

INSTRUCTIONS

Special abbreviations

C4F: Slip next 2sts on to cable needle and hold at front of work, k2 from left needle, then k2 from cable needle.

C4B: Slip next 2sts on to cable needle and hold at back of work, k2 from left needle, then k2 from cable needle.

Cast on a multiple of 22sts plus 3 extra sts.

Row 1 (RS): P3, *k8, p3, rep from *.

Row 2 and all even-numbered (WS) rows: K3, *p8, k3, rep from *.

Row 3: P3, *k8, p3, C4B, C4F, p3, rep from *.

Row 5: Rep row 1.

Row 7: P3, *C4B, C4F, p3, k8, p3, rep from *.

Row 9: Rep row 1.

Rep rows 2–9 to form patt.

GARTER ZIGZAG TWIST

INSTRUCTIONS

Special abbreviations

T2R (twist 2 right): Skip first st on left needle and k 2nd st through front of loop (do not drop st off left needle), then k first st on left needle and drop both sts off left needle at same time.

T2L (twist 2 left): Skip first st on left needle and k 2nd st by taking right needle behind first st to do so (do not drop st off left needle), then k first st on left needle and drop both sts off left needle at same time.

Row 1 (RS): K.
Row 2: *K5, p1, rep from * to last st, k1.
Row 3: K1, *T2L, k4, rep from *.
Row 4: K4, p1, *k5, p1, rep from * to last 2sts, k2.
Row 5: K2, T2L, *k4, T2L, rep from * to last 3sts, k3.
Row 6: K3, p1, *k5, p1, rep from * to last 3sts, k3.
Row 7: K3, T2L, *k4, T2L, rep from * to last 2sts, k2.
Row 8: K2, p1, *k5, p1, rep from * to last 4sts, k4.
Row 9: *K4, T2L, rep from * to last st, k1.
Row 10: K1, *p1, k5, rep from *.
Row 11: *K4, T2R, rep from * to last st, k1.
Row 12: Rep row 8.
Row 13: K3, T2R, *k4, T2R, rep from * to last 2sts, k2.
Row 14: Rep row 6.
Row 15: K2, T2R, *k4, T2R, rep from * to last 3sts, k3.
Row 16: Rep row 4.
Row 17: K1, *T2R, k4, rep from *.
Row 18: Rep row 2.
Rep rows 3–18 to form patt.

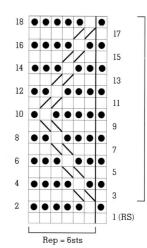

Rep rows 3–18

Rep = 6sts

GARTER STITCH CABLE

INSTRUCTIONS

Special abbreviation

C8F: Place 4sts on cable needle and leave at front of work, k4 from left needle, then k4 from cable needle.

Cast on a multiple of 18sts.
Row 1 (RS): *P5, k8, p5, rep from * to end.
Row 2: *K9, p4, k5, rep from * to end. Rep last 2 rows twice more.
Row 7: *P5, *C8F, p5, rep from * to end.
Row 8: *K5, p4, k9, rep from * to end.
Row 9: As row 1.
Rep last 2 rows four times more, then row 8 again.
Row 19: As row 7.
Row 20: As row 2.
Row 21: As row 1.
Row 22: As row 2.
Row 23: As row 1.
Row 24: As row 2.
Rep rows 1–24 to form pattern.

BOBBLE CABLE

INSTRUCTIONS
Special abbreviations
C8B: Place 4sts on cable needle and leave at back, k4 from left needle, then k4 from cable needle.
MB: Make bobble as follows. (K1, yo) twice, k1, turn, p5, turn, slip 4sts on to right needle, k1, then pass 4 slipped stitches over (one by one), all into next st.

Cast on a multiple of 8sts, plus 4 extra sts.
Row 1: K.
Row 2 and all foll alt rows: P.
Row 3: K.
Row 5: K2, *C8B, rep from * to last 2sts, k2.
Row 7: K2, *MB, k7, rep from * to last 2sts, k2.
Row 9: K.

Row 11: K6, *C8B, rep from * to last 6sts, k6.
Row 13: K6, *MB, k7, rep from * to last 13sts, k13.
Row 14: As row 2.
Rep rows 3–14 to form patt.

6 edge sts   6 edge sts

WOVEN CABLE

INSTRUCTIONS
Special abbreviations
C6F: Place 3sts on cable needle and leave at front of work, k3 from left needle, then k3 from cable needle.
C6B: Place 3sts on cable needle and leave at back of work, k3 from left needle, then k3 from cable needle.

Cast on a multiple of 6sts (a minimum of 12sts).
Row 1 (RS): K.
Row 2 and all foll alt rows: P.
Row 3: K3, *C6B, rep from * to last 3sts, k3.
Row 5: K.
Row 7: *C6F, rep from * to end.

Row 8: As row 2.
Rep rows 1–8 to form patt.

3 edge sts   3 edge sts

CABLE BOXES

INSTRUCTIONS
Special abbreviation
C4F: Place 2sts on cable needle and leave at front of work, k2, then k2 from cable needle.

Cast on a multiple of 8sts plus 4 extra sts.
Row 1 (RS): *P4, k4, rep from * to last 4sts, p4.
Row 2: *K4, p4, k4, rep from *.
Row 3: As row 1.
Row 4: As row 2.
Row 5: *P4, C4F, rep from * to last 4sts, p4.
Rows 6 and 7: As row 2.
Row 8: As row 1.
Row 9: As row 2.
Row 10: As row 1.

Row 11: *C4F, p4, rep from * to last 4sts, C4F.
Row 12: As row 1.
Rep rows 1–12 to form patt.

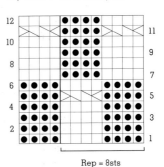

Rep = 8sts

MEDALLION CABLE STITCH

INSTRUCTIONS
Special abbreviations

C4F: Slip next 2sts on to cable needle and hold at front of work, k2 from left needle, then k2 from cable needle.

C4B: Slip next 2sts on to cable needle and hold at back of work, k2 from left needle, then k2 from cable needle.

Cast on a multiple of 22sts plus 3 extra sts.
Row 1 (RS): P3, *k8, p3, rep from *.
Row 2 and all even-numbered (WS) rows: K3, *p8, k3, rep from *.
Row 3: P3, *k8, p3, C4B, C4F, p3, rep from *.

Row 5: P3, *C4B, C4F, p3, k8, p3, rep from *.
Row 7: P3, *k8, p3, C4F, C4B, p3, rep from *.
Row 9: P3, *C4F, C4B, p3, k8, p3, rep from *.
Rep rows 2–9 to form patt.

Rep = 22sts

SIX-STITCH CABLE PATTERN

INSTRUCTIONS
Special abbreviations

C6F: Slip next 3sts on to cable needle and hold at front of work, k3 from left needle, then k3 from cable needle.

C6B: Slip next 3sts on to cable needle and hold at back of work, k3 from left needle, then k3 from cable needle.

Cast on a multiple of 18sts plus 3 extra sts.

Row 1 (RS): P3, *k6, p3, rep from *.
Row 2 and all even-numbered (WS) rows: K3, *p6, k3, rep from *.
Row 3: P3, *k6, p3, C6F, p3, rep from *.
Row 5: Rep row 1.
Row 7: P3, *C6B, p3, k6, p3, rep from *.
Row 9: Rep row 1.
Rep rows 2–9 to form patt.

Rep = 18sts

SMOCKED RIBBING

INSTRUCTIONS
Special abbreviation

smock 5sts: Slip next 5sts on to cable needle and leave at front of work, bring yarn to the front of work, and wrap counterclockwise around these stitches twice so that yarn now sits at back of work. Work (K1, p3, k1) from cable needle.

Cast on a multiple of 8sts, plus 7 extra sts.
Row 1 (RS): P1, k1, *p3, k1, rep from * to last st, p1.
Row 2: K1, p1, *k3, p1, rep from * to last st, k1.

Row 3: P1, smock 5sts, *p3, smock 5sts, rep from * to last st, p1.
Row 4: As row 2.
Row 5: As row 1. Rep last 2 rows once more, and row 2 again.
Row 9: P1, k1, p3, *smock 5sts, p3, rep from * to last 2sts, k1, p1.
Rows 10 and 12: As row 2.
Row 11: As row 1.
Rep rows 1–12 to form pattern.

Colorwork patterns

To make Intarsia patterns less intricate to work, try Swiss Darning (pp. 165–166) in any odd motif stitches afterward.

HEART MOTIF

INSTRUCTIONS
Use the intarsia technique to work this heart. Choose four colors: three motif colors and one background color.

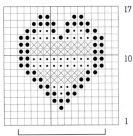

Motif = 13sts wide
(x 14 rows high)

DUCK MOTIF

INSTRUCTIONS
Use the intarsia technique to work this duck motif. Choose four colors: three motif colors and one background color.

Motif = 15sts wide (x 15 rows high)

SNOWFLAKE MOTIF

INSTRUCTIONS
Use the intarsia method to work this motif. Choose two colors: one color for the motif and another for the background.

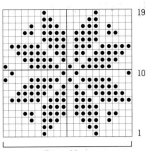

Rep = 20sts

CAT MOTIF

INSTRUCTIONS
Use the intarsia technique to work this cat motif. Choose two colors: one motif color and one background color.

Motif = 20sts wide (x 17 rows high)

BIRD MOTIF

INSTRUCTIONS

Use the intarsia technique to work this bird. Choose five colors: four motif colors and one background color. Work a single motif on the knitting or arrange motifs across the knitting at random intervals or in regular repeating positions.

LITTLE LADY MOTIF

INSTRUCTIONS

Use the intarsia technique to work this motif. Choose eight colors: seven motif colors and one background color. Work a single motif on the knitting or arrange motifs across the knitting at random intervals or in regular repeating positions.

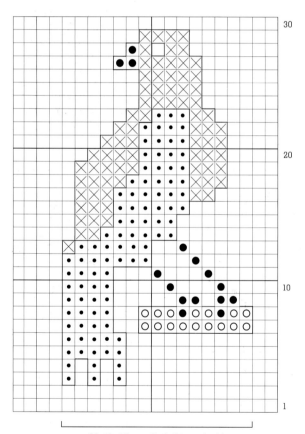

Motif = 15sts wide (x 27 rows high)

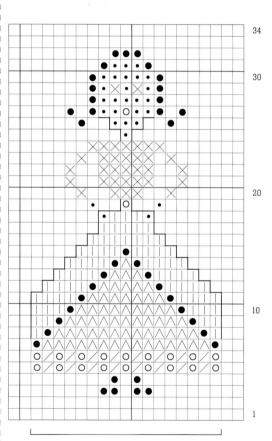

Motif = 17sts wide (x 30 rows high)

SIMPLE BORDERS

INSTRUCTIONS

Use the Fair Isle technique to work these border patterns. Change background and motif colors as desired for each band of pattern.

TULIP MOTIF

INSTRUCTIONS

Use the intarsia technique to work the tulip motif and the background around the tulip head in this pattern. When working the stem, use the Fair Isle technique to work only the background color. Choose four colors: three motif colors and one background color.

REPEATING CIRCLES

INSTRUCTIONS

Use the Fair Isle technique to work this repeating pattern. Choose four colors: two motif colors and two background colors.

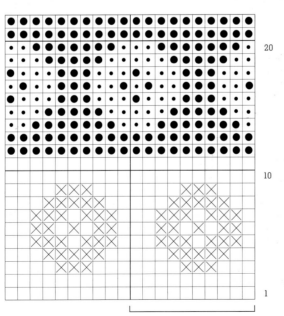

Rep = 10sts (x 22 rows)

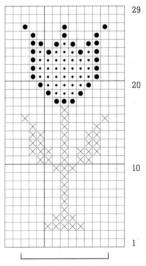

Motif = 11sts wide
(x 25 rows high)

Colorwork patterns **207**

HEARTS

INSTRUCTIONS

Use the Fair Isle technique to work this repeating pattern. Choose two colors: one color for the motif and another color for the background.

Rep = 8sts

FAIR ISLE BLOSSOMS

INSTRUCTIONS

Use the Fair Isle technique to work this repeating pattern. Choose two colors: one motif color and one background color.

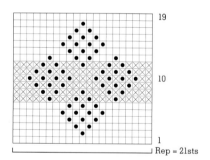

Rep = 8sts wide
(x 8 rows high)

ARGYLE

INSTRUCTIONS

Use the intarsia technique to work the background color and stripe, but strand motif and background/stripe color as Fair Isle behind the argyle motif.

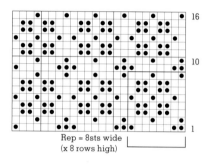

Rep = 21sts

ZIGZAGS

INSTRUCTIONS

Use the three-stranded Fair Isle technique to work this repeating pattern. Choose three colors: a light, medium, and dark shade work best.

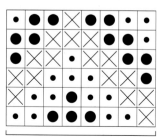

Rep = 8sts

INTARSIA FLOWERS

INSTRUCTIONS

Use the intarsia technique to work the background color around the flowers, but strand both motif and background colors as Fair Isle behind the flowers. To prevent a long background strand in rows 7, 9, 20, and 22, cut the background thread behind the motif leaving long end and beginning threads (temporarily knot together to stop stitches from unraveling), and sew these into the back once the knitting is completed. Choose five colors: two motif colors for each flower and one background color.

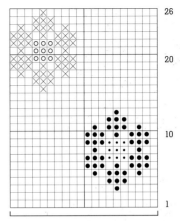

Rep = 20sts (x 26 rows)

NUMBERS AND LETTERS

INSTRUCTIONS

Use the intarsia technique to work the background color and the individual motifs. While working these, strand the background color as Fair Isle behind them.

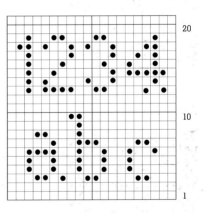

Faux colorwork patterns

PEEPING PURL STITCH

INSTRUCTIONS

Note: All sts to be slipped purlwise.
Using yarn A, cast on an odd number of sts.
Row 1 (RS): Using yarn A, k.
Row 2: Using yarn A, p.
Rows 3 and 4: As rows 1 and 2.
Row 5: Using yarn B, k1, *s1 wyib, k1, rep from * to end.
Row 6: Using yarn B, k1, *s1 wyif, k1, rep from * to end.
Row 7: As row 1.

Row 8: As row 2.
Rep last 2 rows once more.
Row 11: Using yarn B, s1 wyib, *k1, s1 wyib, rep from * to end.
Row 12: Using yarn B, s1 wyif, *k1, s1 wyif, rep from * to end.
Rep rows 2–9 to form patt.

ARROWHEAD STITCH

INSTRUCTIONS
Special abbreviations

C3L: Place one st on cable needle and hold at front of work, k2, then k1 from cable needle.
C3R: Place 2sts on cable needle and hold at back of work, k1, then k2 from cable needle.
Note: All sts to be slipped purlwise. Using yarn A, cast on a multiple of 7sts plus one extra st.
Row 1 (RS): Using yarn A, k.
Row 2: Using yarn A, p.
Rows 3: Using yarn B, *k1, s1 wyib, k4, s1 wyib, rep from * to end.
Row 4: Using yarn B, p1, *s1 wyif, p4, s1 wyif, p1, rep from * to end.
Row 5: Using yarn B, *k1, s1 wyib, k4, s1 wyib, rep from * to end.
Row 6: As row 4.
Row 7: Using yarn B, *k1, C3L, C3R, rep from * to last st, k1.
Row 8: Using yarn B, p.
Row 9: Using yarn A, *k1, s1 wyib, k4, s1 wyib, rep from * to end.
Row 10: Using yarn A, p1, *s1 wyif, p4, s1 wyif, p1, rep from * to end.
Row 11: Using yarn A, *k1, s1 wyib, k4, s1 wyib, rep from * to end.
Row 12: Using yarn A, p1, *s1 wyif, p4, s1 wyif, p1, rep from * to end.
Row 13: Using yarn A, *k1, C3L, C3R, rep from * to last st, k1.
Row 14: Using yarn A, p.
Rep rows 3–14 to form patt.

GARTER SLIP STITCH

INSTRUCTIONS
Note: All sts to be slipped purlwise.
Using yarn C, cast on a multiple of 4sts plus 3 extra sts.
Row 1 (RS): Using yarn A, k1, *s1, k3, rep from * to last 2sts, s1, k1.
Row 2: Using yarn A, k1, *s1 wyif, k3, rep from * to last 2sts, s1 wyif, k1.
Row 3: Using yarn B, k3, *s1, k3, rep from * to end.
Row 4: Using yarn B, k3, *s1 wyif, k3, rep from * to end.
Row 5: Using yarn C, k1, *s1, k3, rep from * to last 2sts, s1, k1.
Row 6: Using yarn C, k1, *s1 wyif, k3, rep from * to last 2sts, s1 wyif, k1.
Row 7: Using yarn A, k3, *s1, k3, rep from * to end.
Row 8: Using yarn A, k3, *s1 wyif, k3, rep from * to end.
Row 9: Using yarn B, k1, *s1, k3, rep from * to last 2sts, s1, k1.
Row 10: Using yarn B, k1, *s1 wyif, k3, rep from * to last 2sts, s1 wyif, k1.
Row 11: Using yarn C, k3, *s1, k3, rep from * to end.
Row 12: Using yarn C, k3, *s1 wyif, k3, rep from * to end.
Rep rows 1–12 to form patt.

WEAVER'S STITCH

INSTRUCTIONS
Note: All sts to be slipped purlwise.
Using yarn A, cast on an even number of sts.
Row 1 (RS): Using yarn A, *k1, s1 wyif, rep from * to end.
Row 2: Using yarn A, *p1, s1 wyib, rep from * to end.
Row 3: Using yarn B, *k1, s1 wyif, rep from * to end.
Row 4: Using yarn B, *p1, s1 wyib, rep from * to end.
Rep rows 1–4 to form patt.

HONEYCOMB STITCH

INSTRUCTIONS

Special abbreviations

C3L: Place one st on cable needle and hold at front of work, k2 from left needle, then k1 from cable needle.
C3R: Place 2sts on cable needle and hold at back of work, k1 from left needle, then k2 from cable needle.
Note: All sts to be slipped purlwise.
Using yarn A, cast on a multiple of 4sts plus one extra st.
Row 1 (RS): Using yarn A, k.
Row 2: Using yarn A, p.
Rows 3: Using yarn B, *s1 wyib, k3, rep from * to last st, s1 wyib.
Row 4: Using yarn B, *s1 wyif, *p3, s1 wyif, rep from * to last st, k1.
Row 5: Using yarn B, *s1 wyib, k3, rep from * to last st, s1 wyib.

Row 6: Using yarn B, *s1 wyif, *p3, s1 wyif, rep from * to last st, k1.
Row 7: Using yarn A, k.
Row 8: Using yarn A, p.
Row 9: Using yarn C, *k2, s1 wyib, k1, rep from * to last st, k1.
Row 10: Using yarn C, p1, *p1, s1 wyif, p2, rep from * to last st, k1.
Row 11: Using yarn C, *k2, s1 wyib, k1, rep from * to last st, k1.
Row 12: Using yarn C, p1, *p1, s1 wyif, p2, rep from * to last st, k1.
Row 13: Using yarn A, k.
Row 14: Using yarn A, p.
Rep rows 3–14 to form patt.

VERTICAL STRIPES

INSTRUCTIONS

Note: All sts to be slipped purlwise. Gauge will be tighter as a result of slipped stitch columns, so it is advisable to cast on three times as many stitches for the width. Using yarn A, cast on a multiple of 4sts.
Row 1 (RS): Using yarn A, k.
Row 2: Using yarn A, p.
Row 3: Using yarn B, k3, s2 wyib, *k2, s2 wyib, rep from * to last 3sts, k3.
Row 4: Using yarn B, p3, s2 wyif, *p2, s2 wyif, rep from * to last 3sts, p3.

Row 5: Using yarn A, k1, s2 wyib, *k2, s2, rep from * to last st, k1.
Row 6: Using yarn A, p1, s2 wyif, *p2, s2 wyif, rep from * to last st, p1.
Rep rows 3–6 to form patt.

BROKEN STRIPES

INSTRUCTIONS

Note: All sts to be slipped purlwise.
Using yarn A, cast on a multiple of 4sts plus 2 extra sts.
Row 1 (RS): Using yarn A, k.
Row 2: Using yarn A, p.
Rows 3 and 4: As rows 1 and 2.
Row 5: Using yarn B, k2, *s1, k3, rep from * to end.
Row 6: Using yarn B, p.

Row 7: Using yarn B, k.
Row 8: Using yarn B, p.
Row 9: Using yarn A, k4, *s1, k3, rep from * to last 2sts, s1, k1.
Rep rows 2–9 to form patt.

Edging patterns

OPEN WEAVE EDGING

INSTRUCTIONS

Cast on a multiple of 6sts plus one extra st.
Row 1 (RS): K.
Row 2: P.
Row 3: *[K1, p1, k1, p1, k1] into next st, k5tog, rep from * to end.

Row 4: P.
Rep rows 1–4 to form patt.

BEADED EDGING

INSTRUCTIONS

Prethread the beads and push them down the yarn until you are instructed to use them.
Cast on 6sts.
Rows 1 and 2 (RS): K.
Row 3: Push 10 beads up the working yarn and press against first presenting stitch on left needle.

k1 tbl, k to end as normal, leaving bead loop in place.
Rows 4, 5, and 6: K.
Rep rows 1–6 to form patt.

PEAKS EDGING

INSTRUCTIONS

Cast on 6sts.
Row 1 and all odd-numbered (RS) rows: K.
Row 2: Yo, k2, k2tog, yo, k2. (7sts)
Row 4: Yo, k3, k2tog, yo, k2. (8sts)
Row 6: Yo, k4, k2tog, yo, k2. (9sts)
Row 8: Yo, k5, k2tog, yo, k2. (10sts)
Row 10: Yo, k6, k2tog, yo, k2. (11sts)
Row 12: Yo, s1 k2tog psso, k4, k2tog, yo, k2. (10sts)
Row 14: Yo, s1 k2tog psso, k3, k2tog, yo, k2. (9sts)
Row 16: Yo, s1 k2tog psso, k2, k2tog, yo, k2. (8sts)

Row 18: Yo, s1 k2tog psso, k1, k2tog, yo, k2. (7sts)
Row 20: Yo, s1 k2tog psso, k2tog, yo, k2. (6sts)
Rep rows 1–20 until edging is desired length, ending with a row 20.
Cast off knitwise.

CHRISTENING EDGING

INSTRUCTIONS

Cast on 7sts.
Row 1 (RS): K2, yo, k2tog, yo twice, k2tog, k1. (8sts)
Row 2: K3, p1, k2, yo, k2tog.
Row 3: K2, yo, k2tog, k1, yo twice, k2tog, k1. (9sts)
Row 4: K3, p1, k3, yo, k2tog.

Row 5: K2, yo, k2tog, k2, yo twice, k2tog, k1. (10sts)
Row 6: K3, p1, k4, yo, k2tog.
Row 7: K2, yo, k2tog, k6.
Row 8: Cast off 3sts knitwise, k4, yo, k2tog. (7sts)
Rep rows 1–8 until edging is desired length, ending with a row 8.
Cast off knitwise.

ARCHWAY EDGING

INSTRUCTIONS

All stitches are cast on using the backward loop cast-on method (see p. 35).

Cast on a multiple of 6sts plus 2 extra sts.

Row 1 (RS): K.

Row 2: *K1, cast off 3sts, rep from * to end.

Row 3: K1, *cast on one st, k2, rep from * to last st, cast on one st, k1.

Rows 4, 5, and 6: K.

PICOT RUFFLE EDGING

INSTRUCTIONS

Note: This edging is worked widthwise.

Cast on an odd number of sts.

Row 1 (RS): K.

Row 2: K.

Row 3: *K2tog, yo, rep from * to last st, k1.

Rows 4, 5, and 6: K.

Row 7: K1, *[k1, p1, k1] into next st, [k1, p1] into next st, rep from *. (This row increases the number of stitches on the needle by about two and a half times.)

Row 8: P.

Row 9: K.

Rows 10, 11, 12, and 13: [Rep rows 8 and 9] twice.

Row 14 (WS): P.

Rows 15 and 16: K.

Work picots along cast-off as follows:

Picot cast-off: *Cast on 2sts on left needle using knit-on cast-on method, cast off 5sts knitwise, transfer st on right needle back to left needle, rep from *, ending last cast-off as required by sts remaining.

FRINGE EDGING

INSTRUCTIONS

Note: When making this edging, hold 2 strands of yarn together throughout and knit tightly. You can alter the length of fringe by adding to or subtracting from number of knit stitches at end of row 1 and adjusting purl stitches at beg of row 2 by same number.

Cast on 12sts.

Row 1 (RS): K2, yo, k2tog, k8.

Row 2: P7, k2, yo, k2tog, k1.

Rep rows 1 and 2 until edging is desired length, ending with a row 2.

Cast off (RS): Cast off first 5sts knitwise, cut yarn and draw through loop on right needle to fasten off, then drop rem 6sts off left needle and unravel them to form fringe.

Smooth out unraveled strands, and, if necessary, lightly steam to straighten the strands. Then cut through loops at end of fringe. Knot strands together in groups of four strands, positioning knots close to edge of knitting. Trim fringe ends slightly, if necessary, to make them even.

PETAL EDGING

INSTRUCTIONS

Cast on 6sts.

Row 1 (RS): K.

Row 2: Yo, k2, k2tog, yo, k2. (7sts)

Row 3: K.

Row 4: Yo, k to last 4sts, k2tog, yo, k2. (8sts)

Rows 5–10: (Rep rows 3 and 4) three times. (11sts)

Row 11: K.

Row 12: Cast off 5sts loosely knitwise, k1, k2tog, yo, k2. (6sts)

Rep rows 1–12 until edging is desired length, ending with a row 12.

Cast off knitwise.

Beading stitch patterns

SUBTLE SPARKLES

INSTRUCTIONS

Special abbreviation

pb: Place bead.

Cast on a multiple of 6sts plus 2 extra sts.

Row 1 (RS): K.
Row 2: P.
Row 3: K1, *pb, k5, rep from * to last st, k1.
Row 4: P.

Row 5: K.
Row 6: P.
Row 7: K1, *k3, pb, k2, rep from * to last st, k1.
Row 8: P.

Rep rows 1–8 to form patt.

DIAGONAL BEADING

INSTRUCTIONS

Special abbreviation

pb: Place bead.

Cast on a multiple of 5sts plus 2 extra sts.

Row 1: K1, *k2, pb, k2, rep from * to last st, k1.
Row 2 and all foll alt rows: P.
Row 3: K1, *k1, pb, k3, rep from * to last st, k1.
Row 5: K1, *pb, k4, rep from * to last st, k1.

Row 7: K1, *k4, pb, rep from * to last st, k1.
Row 9: K1, *k3, pb, rep from * to last st, k1.
Row 10: P.

Rep rows 1–10 to form patt.

BEADED STOCKINETTE STITCH

INSTRUCTIONS

Special abbreviation

pb: Place bead.

Cast on an odd number of sts.

Row 1: K1, *pb, k1, rep from * to end.
Row 2: P.
Row 3: *K1, pb, rep from * to last st, k1.

Row 4: P.

Rep rows 1–4 to form patt.

BEADED CHECKERBOARD

INSTRUCTIONS

Special abbreviation

pb: Place bead.

Cast on a multiple of 10sts plus 7 extra sts.

Row 1 (RS): K1, *[pb, k1] three times, k4, rep from * to last 6sts, [pb, k1] three times.
Row 2 and all foll alt rows: P.
Rows 3: K2, *[pb, k1] twice, k6, rep from * to last 5sts, [pb, k1] twice, k1.

Row 5: As row 1.
Row 7: K6, *[pb, k1] three times, k4, rep from * to last 5sts, k to end.
Row 9: K7, *[pb, k1] twice, k6, rep from * to end.
Row 11: As row 7.

Rep rows 1–12 to form patt.

PEEKABOO BEADS

INSTRUCTIONS
Special abbreviation
pb: Place bead.

Cast on a multiple of 10sts plus 5 extra sts.
Row 1 (RS): K.
Row 2: P1, *k3, p7, rep from * to last 4sts, k3, p1.
Row 3: K2, *pb, k9, rep from * to last 2sts, k2.
Row 4: P.

Row 5: K.
Row 6: P6, *k3, p7, rep from * to last 9sts, k3, p to end.
Row 7: K7, *pb, k9, rep from * to last 8sts, pb, k7.
Row 8: P.
Rep rows 1–8 to form patt.

BEADED GARTER STITCH

INSTRUCTIONS
Special abbreviation
pb: Place bead.

Cast on an odd number of sts.
Row 1 (RS): K.
Row 2, 4, and 6: K.
Rows 3: K1, *pb, k1, rep from * to end.
Row 5: K.
Rep rows 1–6 to form patt.

DIAMANTÉ STITCH

INSTRUCTIONS
Special abbreviation
pb: Place bead.

Cast on a multiple of 8sts plus 2 extra sts.
Row 1 (RS): K1, *k1, pb, k3, pb, k2, rep from * to last st, k1.
Row 3: K1, *k4, pb, k1, pb, k1, rep from * to last st, k1.

Row 5: K1, *k1, pb, k3, pb, k2, rep from * to last st, k1.
Row 7: K1, *pb, k1, pb, k5, rep from * to last st, k1.
Row 8: P.
Rep rows 1–8 to form patt.

VERTICAL SEQUIN STRIPES

INSTRUCTIONS
Special abbreviation
pb: Place bead—sequin.

Cast on a multiple of 8sts plus one extra st.
Row 1: K1, *k2, pb, k1, pb, k3, rep from * to end.
Row 2: P.
Rep rows 1 and 2 to form patt.

Beading stitch patterns **215**

Glossary

Aran yarn
Also called medium, 12-ply, worsted, or Afghan (yarn symbol 4). A medium yarn suitable for sweaters, cabled menswear, blankets, hats, scarves, and mittens.

Backstitch
A sewing stitch used for firm, straight seams that is worked from the wrong side.

Ballband
The wrapper around a ball of yarn that usually details fiber content, weight, length, needle size, gauge, and cleaning instructions.

Ball-winder
A device for winding hanks of yarn into balls; also to wind two or more strands together to make a double-stranded yarn. Often used in conjunction with a swift.

Bias knitting
Diagonally shaped pieces of knitting that slope either to the left or the right.

Blocking
The finishing process for a piece of knitting in which it is set in shape using water or steam.

Bulky or chunky yarn
Also called 14-ply, craft, or rug (yarn symbol 5). A chunky yarn suitable for rugs, jackets, blankets, hats, leg warmers, and winter accessories.

Cable
A design made by crossing one or more stitches over other stitches in a row; it frequently resembles a rope or cable. Twist stitches belong to the same family.

Cable cast-on
A method of casting on that gives a neat, defined edge, producing a firm, cord-like hem.

Cable needle
A needle with a kink or U-shape, used when working cables.

Casting off /binding off
Completing a piece of knitting by finishing off the loops of the stitches so that they cannot unravel.

Casting on
Forming an initial number of stitches on a needle at the start of a piece of knitting. There are various methods, depending on the effect you want to achieve.

Circular knitting
Working on circular needles or double-pointed needles to produce a seamless item such as a hat. There is no need to turn the work and no wrong-side row. Sometimes called tubular knitting.

Circular needles
A pair of short needles connected by a flexible tube, usually used for circular knitting and very wide projects that do not fit on conventional straight needles.

Colorwork
Any method of incorporating color into your knitting. This includes stripes, Fair Isle, intarsia, and slipped stitch patterns.

Continental-style knitting
A way of holding the yarn as you knit, lacing it around your left hand and using these fingers to position the yarn to make a stitch.

Darning in ends
The process of completing a piece of knitting by weaving yarn ends (such as from the cast-on and cast-off edges) into the knitting to disguise them.

Decreases/decreasing
Techniques that subtract stitches. Used to shape knitting and to form textures in combination with other stitches.

Double cast-on
See **Two-strand cast-on** and **Long-tail cast-on**.

Double-knit yarn (DK)
A medium-weight yarn. Also called DK, 5–6-ply, or light worsted (yarn symbol 3). A light yarn suitable for sweaters, lightweight scarves, blankets, and toys.

Double-pointed needles
Knitting needles with a tip at each end; a set of four or five is used for the circular knitting of small items, such as mittens and socks.

Double-sided or double knitting.
See **tubular knitting**.

English-style knitting
A way of holding the yarn as you knit, lacing it around your right hand and using the right forefinger to wrap the yarn around the needle.

Fair Isle patterns
Various multicolored, stranded, geometric patterns originating from Fair Isle and latterly the Shetland Islands in Scotland.

Fair Isle knitting
A method in which yarn colors not being worked are carried across the back of the work until required. This unworked yarn can also be woven in.

Faux colorwork
Adding yarn in another color without having to knit with two different yarns in each row. It involves manipulating stitches from previous rows.

Fibers
Yarn is made up of fibers, such as the hair from an animal, man-made (synthetic) fibers, or fibers derived from a plant. The fibers are processed and spun into a yarn.

Fine yarn
Also called 4-ply, sport, or baby (yarn symbol 2). A fine yarn suitable for lightweight sweaters, babywear, socks, and accessories.

Fisherman's rib
A pattern of knit and purl stitches, in which alternating stitches are double knitted, making a thick, warm, textured fabric.

Fully fashioned shaping
An attractive method for increasing or decreasing when working stockinette stitch, in which a line of stitches is preserved to follow the edge of the piece.

Garter stitch
Working in knit stitches on every row, whichever side of the knitting is facing you. It produces a thick fabric, which is identical on both sides and will not curl at the edges.

Gauge square
A square knitted to the required number of stitches and rows to match the stated gauge of a project, usually 4in (10cm) square. A knitter must achieve the gauge stated in a pattern, or else the knitted item will not end up the correct size.

Hank
A twisted ring of yarn, which needs to be wound into one or more balls before it can be used.

I-cord
A narrow tube of knitting, created on a knitting dolly or cord-maker, or knitted on double-pointed needles. Used as cords, straps, ties, or as a trimming.

Increases/increasing
Creating stitches during knitting. Can be combined with other stitches in order to form shapes and textures.

Intarsia
A method for working with different colored yarns to create blocks of color. A separate length of yarn is used for each color of the motif and twisted where the color changes to prevent a hole; yarns are not stranded across the reverse of the work. Uses less yarn than Fair Isle knitting.

Knit-on cast-on
This cast-on uses two needles to combine a cast-on with the knitting of the first row. If worked through the front of the loops, it produces a soft edge; if through the back of the loops, the edge is firmer.

Knit stitch
One of the two basic stitches used to form knitting.

Knitting beads
Beads with a central hole in various sizes for specific thicknesses of yarn. Most are washable and colorfast.

Knitting needle gauge
A tool for identifying needle size by pushing it through holes.

Knitting through back of loop
Stitches that twist the stitch in the row below so that the legs of the stitch cross at the base.

Knitwise
Working with knit stitches facing you, inserting the right-hand needle into a stitch as if to knit it. See also **Purlwise**.

Lanolin
An oily substance contained in sheep's wool.

Live stitches
Stitches that are currently being worked.

Long-tail cast-on method
See also two-strand cast-on. This method is also known as a double cast-on. It produces a sturdy, reinforced edge and so is good for ribbing.

Mattress stitch
A seaming stitch, which is almost invisible, used to sew pieces of knitting together with the right side facing. It forms only a small seam on the wrong side of the work.

Medallion
A circular, hexagonal, octagonal, or square flat shape made of knitting that is knitted from the center outward.

Mercerized cotton
Cotton thread, fabric, or yarn that has been treated in order to strengthen it and add a sheen. The yarn is a good choice for items that need to be strong and hold a shape, such as a bag.

Organic wool
Wool produced from sheep that graze on land that is not treated with herbicides, pesticides, or artificial fertilizers. The wool is not given any man-made chemical treatments.

Pilling
When the surface of a knitted item rubs up into tiny balls, due to wear and friction.

Plied yarn
A yarn made from more than one strand of spun fiber. Although 4-ply means four strands plied together, it does not necessarily indicate the thickness of the final yarn. Most knitting yarns are plied, as plying prevents the yarn from twisting and the resulting fabric from knitting diagonally.

Purl stitch
One of the two basic stitches used in knitting.

Purlwise
Working with stitches facing you, inserting the right-hand needle into a stitch as if to purl it. See also **Knitwise**.

Put-up
A specific quantity of yarn packaged for sale, such as a ball, hank, or skein.

Ribbing/rib/rib stitch
Knitting with great elasticity, used where fabric needs to hold tightly to the body but is capable of expanding. Single ribbing or 1 x 1 rib is knit 1, purl 1; 2 x 2 rib is knit 2, purl 2; 3 x 3 rib is knit 3, purl 3 etc.

Short-row shaping
Used for shaping shoulders, curving hems, making darts, and turning sock heels. Rows are added in only one part of the fabric by knitting part of a row instead of knitting it to the end. It uses one of three turning methods to close holes.

Single-strand cast-on
A group of methods for casting on using one strand of yarn. Tends to produce a soft edge, but this can be made firmer by twisting the stitches.

Skein
Yarn sold wound into a long oblong shape that is ready to knit.

Slip knot
A knot that you form when you place the first loop on the needle as you start casting on stitches.

Slip stitch
Sliding a stitch from the left-hand needle to the right-hand needle without working it. The usual method is to slip stitches purlwise; less frequently, stitches are slipped knitwise. Slipped stitches at the beginning of each row—slipped selvage—can help to create a very neat edge.

Sock blocker
A flat plastic or wooden shape that is inserted into a finished sock and used to mold it to shape in conjunction with moisture.

Stockinette stitch
A stitch formed by knitting all stitches when the right side of the work is facing you, and purling all stitches when the wrong side of the work is facing you.

Stranded beading method
A process for streamlining the knitting-in of beads by threading them on yarn before you begin, using a needle and thread looped through the yarn. Beads are later arranged in the knitting when brought to the front of the work and wrapped around a slipped stitch.

Super bulky or super chunky yarn
Also called 16-ply (and upward), bulky, or roving (yarn symbol 6). A chunky yarn suitable for heavy blankets, rugs, and thick scarves.

Superfine yarn
Also called 3-ply, fingering, or baby (yarn symbol 1). A very fine yarn suitable for fine-knit socks, shawls, and babywear.

Swift
A wooden frame used with a ball-winder to transform a hank of yarn into convenient balls.

Tape yarn
A wide, flat, or tubular yarn, flattened when wound into a ball. Can be knitted to produce a nubbly or smooth result.

Three-needle cast-off /bind-off
A method of casting off that binds two sets of stitches together while casting off simultaneously. This creates a firm, neat seam with a smooth finish on the right side of the work. It is a good way of finishing the toe of a sock or the fingertip area of a mitten.

Tubular cast-on/cast-off
Also known as an invisible cast-on/off. Produces a good edge for a single rib; best to use needles that are at least two sizes smaller than the main fabric to prevent the ribbing from stretching out of shape.

Tubular knitting
Also known as double knitting or double-sided knitting. It is worked on straight needles by slipping every other stitch and produces a double-sided fabric. See also **Circular knitting**.

Tunisian knitting
A style of knitting where the finished fabric resembles crocheted work.

Twist
Two stitches twisted together to form a narrow cable, which slants to the right or left. A cable needle is not used.

Two-strand cast-on
A group of methods for casting on using two strands of yarn. Tends to produce a strong, elastic edge.

Whipstitch
Stitch used to seam two pieces of knitting by placing them right sides together and then sewing through the edge stitches. Also called oversewing or overcasting.

Yarn
Fibers that have been spun into a long strand in order for you to knit with them. Yarns may be made of natural fibers, man-made fibers, a blend of the two, or even non-standard materials.

Yarn bobbins
Small plastic shapes for holding yarn when doing intarsia work, where there are many yarns in different colors.

Yarn over (yo)
An instruction to increase by adding stitches and creating holes at the same time. There are various situations in which one can create a yarn over: yarn over between knit stitches; yarn over between purl stitches; yarn over between knit and purl stitches; and yarn over at the beginning of a row. .

Index

Acknowledgments

About the author

Vikki Haffenden is a professional knitted textiles designer with a background in commercial knitwear design. She currently teaches in knitted textiles at the University of Brighton. Vikki recently co-authored *The Knitting Book* (2011), and her work has been featured in a number of hand knitting publications. Acting as design consultant she contributed to the development of Rooster hand-knit yarns and the *Rooster Pattern Book One* (2005–2006). Vikki is the author of *Double-bed Machine Knitting Explained* (1997), and has just completed a practice-based research Doctorate into industrial, electronic machine knitting and its relationships with larger sized body shape. Her flexible and enthusiastic design practice in both hand and machine knitting has led to Vikki developing a depth of knowledge and understanding about knitting that is truly unique.

Frederica Patmore, author of the tools and materials, projects, and stitch pattern chapters, is a Design Consultant for Rowan Yarns, one of the biggest providers of luxury yarns in the world. She runs a number of classes at different skill levels in branches of the John Lewis department store in the UK and independent knitting shops, and contributes to needlecraft publications. In addition to being a master of knitting technique, Frederica is an accomplished and successful knitting pattern designer.

Acknowledgments

Vikki Haffenden
It has given me great pleasure to work on this book with the editorial staff at Dorling Kindersley. Particular thanks go to Penny Smith for her constant support throughout. I also wish to express my gratitude to my wonderful family: Ross, Jack, Ben, and Tom, for their patience and understanding while I pursue my passion for knitting in all its sumptuous depth and detail. Without them I would have foundered at the first chapter. Finally, I would like to acknowledge the talented knitters past and present who have motivated me to pursue a career in knitting and to aspire to bring this book to you.

Frederica Patmore
I would like to thank Rowan Yarns for all their support with fabulous yarns and garments, especially Sarah and Sharon, the Kidsilk Queens. A very special thank you to all my wonderful knitters and pattern checkers—such amazing hands you all have! Finally, a huge thank you to DK, you've been a joy to work with.

Dorling Kindersley would like to thank:
Rose Sharp Jones for her exemplary technical assistance for the photoshoot and help on the new additional project added to the section. Rachel Vowles for the amazing job she did checking that all the stitch patterns were correct. Dorothy Kikon and Becky Alexander for editorial assistance. Irene Lyford for proofreading and Dr. Laurence Errington for indexing.